FLORIDA

in

WORLD WAR II

FLORIDA
in
WORLD WAR II

FLOATING FORTRESS

NICK WYNNE &
RICHARD MOORHEAD

Charleston · London

THE
History
PRESS

Published by The History Press
Charleston, SC 29403
www.historypress.net

First published 2010
Second printing 2012

Manufactured in the United States

ISBN 978.1.59629.929.0

Library of Congress Cataloging-in-Publication Data

Wynne, Nick.
Florida in World War II : floating fortress / Nick Wynne and Richard Moorhead.
p. cm.
Includes bibliographical references.
ISBN 978-1-59629-929-0
1. World War, 1939-1945--Florida. 2. Florida--History, Military--20th century. 3. Florida-
-History--20th century. I. Moorhead, Richard, 1943- II. Title. III. Title: Florida in World
War 2. IV. Title: Florida in World War Two.
D769.85.F5W96 2010
940.54'127309759--dc22
2010015316

For Debra and Lisa Wynne

For Sandy Moorhead

Contents

CONTENTS

ACKNOWLEDGEMENTS

W riting a book is never a singular task. There are many people who make researching and writing a pleasure when they offer suggestions, point the authors to new sources or generously share their research. Florida is blessed to have a number of local and statewide scholars, professionals and talented laypersons whose objective in life is not to hoard information for unwritten books but to share their resources with individuals who are actively writing. Their concern is that the "Florida story" in its entirety be put before the public. They are silent, unseen coauthors on many books, and they certainly are coauthors of *Florida in World War II: Floating Fortress.* This is "our" book, collectively.

Special thanks go out to Peggy Ryals, a dear high school friend from Myrtle Beach, whose passion for English grammar and history makes her a willing and valuable person to pass an unedited chapter to. We always anxiously await her judgments. While we don't always use her suggestions (yes, we know we have a propensity to split infinitives), they are all important. June Geiger, whose brother, Hal Gettings, was one of the original thirteen members of the naval detachment that built Banana River Naval Air Station in 1939, is also an important commentator whose red pen is always sharp.

Greg Parsons, curator of the Camp Blanding Museum, and retired Sergeant Major Craig Petelle helped us immensely by discovering information and pictures about this base and the men who trained there during World War II. Dr. David Coles, history professor at Longwood College in Virginia, contributed—although he wasn't aware of it—with information he collected and posted on history websites while he was employed by the State of Florida. Rebecca A. Saunders, the local history expert in the Bay County Library System, provided information and pictures about the Wainwright Shipyard in Panama City. Claude W. Bass III, the voice of Clay County history, provided rare pictures of Lee Field (Green Cove Springs Naval Air Station). Jack Rabun and Ada E. Parrish allowed us to use their postcard collections as illustrations. Irv Rubin, retired B-24 pilot, has given his collection of World War II materials to the Florida Historical Society, and it provided a great deal of information. Retired colonel Mike Nix, another high school classmate, put us in touch with important sources at Eglin Air Force Base (AFB), where he currently works as a civilian in the defense industry. Clay T. McCutchan, Air Armaments Center historian at Eglin AFB, provided very good information on the history of Eglin AFB, along with a guided tour of the historical sites. Carol Goad, curator at the Sebring Historical Society's library, allowed us to select and copy photographs from its holdings. Kathy Couturier, cultural resource manager and archaeologist at Avon Park Air Force Range, generously donated her time to scan old photographs for us. Ashley Miller of the Brevard County Historical Commission found and copied photographs on the Melbourne Naval Air Station (NAS) for us. The staff at the Beaches Area Museum and Historical Society at Jacksonville Beach willingly shared their collection of materials and pictures about the Ponte Vedra saboteurs. That was a godsend.

The staff of the Special Collections Department at the University of South Florida, the staff of the Tampa Bay History Center, the staff of the Tampa-Hillsborough Public Library System and Stephanie Gaub and the staff of the Orange County Regional History Center supplied pictures and pointed us in new directions. Ruth McSween of the National Navy UDT-SEAL Museum in Fort Pierce provided pictures and research material; so, too, did Pam Cooper at the Indian River Public Library in Vero Beach. Neal Adam Watson of the Florida Photographic Archives responded rapidly to requests for copies of photographs from the massive files of that state agency. Retired veteran Frank Towers, who is a volunteer at the Camp Blanding Museum, also provided wonderful stories and firsthand accounts of life as a trainee at the post during the early 1940s. Special thanks to Theo Elbert, a volunteer at the Emil Buehler Aviation Museum in Pensacola, and to Gina Marini and Cynthia Tomberlin at the Heritage Museum of Valparaiso.

The staff of the Camp Gordon Johnston Museum and the hundreds of veterans who trained at that base during the war gave us new insight into the place known as "Hell by the Sea." We were fortunate enough to attend their reunion on March 12 and 13, 2010. Little remains of that camp now, but the memories of these members of the "greatest generation" remain fresh. Linda Minichiello, curator of the Gordon Johnston Museum, was a great help in providing pictures and information about the 100,000 men who occupied and trained at this base, which was only active from 1942 to 1945 before it was bulldozed into oblivion in early 1946.

There are many more people, too numerous to mention, who contributed to this volume. Thank you all very much!

Introduction

WORLD WAR II AND ITS IMPACT ON THE SUNSHINE STATE

In 2011, Americans will observe the seventieth anniversary of the entry of the United States into World War II. Sadly, the more than 16 million men and women who made up the nation's armed forces during that war are dying at the rate of 1,000 per day, and soon there will be no more. Of the multitudes who made up the soldiers, sailors and flyers of the American military in the 1940s, some 248,000 came from the Sunshine State. Their contributions, like those of other Americans, were vital to the success of the nation and its allies. This "greatest generation" certainly deserves to be recognized for its sacrifices and service.

"They also serve" became a popular slogan to portray the contributions of the millions of Americans on the homefront. From working in war industries to buying war bonds, from conducting scrap metal drives to enduring rationing and from volunteering to entertain service personnel in hospitals and USOs (United Service Organizations) to providing service as air raid wardens and much more, the civilian population made vast contributions to the war effort. Like their fellow citizens, Floridians also served.

Historians frequently talk about defining moments in history when events cause changes—temporary at first, but soon becoming permanent. For the Sunshine State and its people, World War II was a defining moment. Florida after 1941 was radically different from the Florida that existed before that date. Suffering from the ill effects of the land boom collapse in the mid-1930s and the Great Depression, prewar Florida was a typical agrarian southern state where almost 80.00 percent of its population lived in rural areas or small towns and depended on some form of agriculture—citrus farming, cattle ranching, truck farming, tobacco or cotton cultivation, lumbering or naval stores collection—for a living. By 1942, Florida's population had become largely urban, a change brought about by the demand for workers of all kinds for war industries and by the influx of large numbers of job seekers from surrounding states (a trend that continues today). In the 1950 census, only 19.06 percent of Floridians were listed as living in rural areas. Those who migrated from Florida's countryside seldom returned to it after the war. The Sunshine State moved from being predominantly rural in nature to becoming an urban-oriented state.

Many of those who came to the state looking for work or who were stationed here in the military stayed or returned, and in 1950, the permanent population of the state was recorded at 2.8 million, up from the 1.9 million recorded in 1940. The population growth stimulated by the war continued unabated in the following years. Florida was the South's least-populated state in 1940, but by 1990, just fifty years later, it had become the fourth most populous state in the Union. By 2000, more than 80.0 million temporary visitors joined its 18.5 million permanent residents each year.

For individual Floridians, whose annual incomes were only $308 in 1940, the war produced immediate results. By 1950, individual incomes in the Sunshine State averaged $1,018. Much of the increase in average income was due to the wages paid to workers in war industries or at military installations. Although rationing restricted the numbers and amounts of items available for purchase, Floridians found ways around rationing. Expanding manufacturing demanded more and more workers, and wages accelerated accordingly.

For women, World War II brought significant change in their social and economic status. For white women, the demand for labor allowed them to move out of offices and onto factory floors. By 1943, white women made up about 25 percent of the total workforce in Florida's war industries, and they were particularly visible in the shipyards of the state as welders, shop supervisors and designers. By 1945, they were performing virtually every job previously performed by men. Federal contracts encouraged the use of women, senior citizens and handicapped persons as employees, and employers proved willing to abide by these mandates.

African American women, however, failed to gain footholds in factories and remained largely relegated to domestic work. Although segregated, African American women served in a number of volunteer organizations such as the Red Cross and the USO. In addition, a few black women were admitted into the WAVES (Women Accepted for Volunteer Emergency Service), WAC (Women's Army Corps) and other female military services.

Some African American men did find work in factories and shipyards, although they were paid less per day and filled mostly menial jobs. While government contracts did not list African Americans as a minority or call for their inclusion in the workforce, the tremendous pressure to meet deadlines and quotas made it essential to include them. Given a choice between staunchly upholding the Jim Crow system and losing jobs for whites, compromises were made. Even though discrimination in the workplace did lessen somewhat in Florida, the practices of a segregated society continued. Many African Americans left the state to seek work in factories in the North, where more opportunities existed.

African Americans also served in the various branches of the military. Of the quarter million men and women from the Sunshine State who served, fifty thousand were African Americans. Once in service, however, blacks were segregated into separate units. At Camp Blanding, for example, African American troops—designated Detachment 2—were bivouacked in an area located between white troops and German-Italian prisoners of war. Early in the war, Selective Service boards refused to call up African Americans on an equal footing as whites. On February 17, 1943, Paul V. McNutt, chairman of the War Manpower Commission, addressed this disparity in a letter to General Lewis B. Hershey, head of the Selective Service, as well as to the secretary of war and the secretary of the navy. McNutt reminded the men that the Selective Training and Service Act of 1940 prohibited racial discrimination in the draft, but the "admission of Negroes into the armed forces has been exercised by severe limitations on the numbers permitted to enlist." Although African Americans made up 10 percent of the population, they constituted less "than six percent of our armed forces." The failure to include more black men in service, he warned, created a potentially dangerous legal problem, "as the single white registrants disappear and husbands and fathers become the current white inductees, while single Negro registrants who are physically fit remain uninducted."

However, changes for African Americans were coming. The exemplary record of service by African Americans made it more difficult to maintain a segregated American society, and in 1948, President Harry S Truman ordered the desegregation of the American armed services. Within the next two decades, every legal vestige of the Jim Crow system disappeared from American society. It was slow in coming, perhaps, but constituted an achievement that can be traced directly to the impact of World War II.

There were other changes for the people of Florida that can be traced to the war. During the first three years of the war, more than fifteen hundred miles of new highways were built, the first producing oil well was drilled in Collier County, DDT was used on a widespread basis to bring mosquitoes and other biting bugs under control, permanent new industries were established and prospered and, most of all, Floridians moved past the rigid religious mentality that governed most southern states and emerged as an urbane and sophisticated society with only nominal southern roots.

Florida in World War II: Floating Fortress is an attempt to look at all aspects of World War II and its impact on the people of Florida. Invariably, we will miss noting some important event or locale, and for that, we apologize. We hope the reader will accept this book in the way we wrote it—as a wonderful, exciting and information-filled exploration of a generation of people who worked, fought and died to protect and improve our country. The Floridians who contributed to the success of the Allied forces in World War II truly are a part of the "greatest generation."

Chapter I

CLOUDY SKIES IN THE SUNSHINE STATE

Prewar Florida

This great Nation will endure as it has endured, will revive and will prosper. So, first of all, let me assert my firm belief that the only thing we have to fear is fear itself—nameless, unreasoning, unjustified terror which paralyzes needed efforts to convert retreat into advance.
—*Franklin Delano Roosevelt, 1933*

G od must love the common man," Abraham Lincoln once said. "He made so many of them." Florida in the 1930s was very much the land of the common man and bore little resemblance to the Sunshine State of the 1920s, when everybody of any importance came to see and be seen. The land boom, which had fueled the economy for more than half a decade, was moribund by 1927, and the collapse of the state's banking system, which had provided easy credit, was the coup de grâce to its foundering economy. Raw land, once a commodity worth untold millions, lay fallow, occasionally pockmarked by empty subdivisions awaiting optimistic builders to construct new homes for phantom buyers who never came. The annual migration of tourists, long considered as predictable as the yearly flights of wild birds, slowed to a standstill, while the millions of dollars they brought with them diminished to a mere trickle. Although Miami and Palm Beach still maintained a façade of the hurly-burly of the previous decade, hoteliers found it necessary to offer deeply discounted rates to attract paying customers. The advertising mills still turned out brochures that featured the high jinks of the wealthy cavorting on beaches or partying in casinos and nightclubs, but the volume of such advertisements—once a raging torrent of paper and pictures—slowed and gradually dried up as profit margins decreased. Even in these once fabled playgrounds, changes were in the air.

In Carl Fisher's Miami Beach and Glenn Curtiss's Hialeah, the nation's criminal element, led by the notorious Alphonse "Scarface Al" Capone, now ruled. Movie stars and sports figures, among South Florida's major attractions, still came to Miami, but not in the numbers they once did. In Palm Beach, scions of established fortunes and their families withdrew to their mansions in compounds hidden behind walls of sea grapes and coquina, safe from the envious eyes of the common man, whom many feared might just embrace a revolutionary approach to resolving the disparity between America's rich and poor.

Across the peninsula, Floridians hunkered down, trying to salvage what they could from the halcyon days of the Florida boom. While the state might have returned to the control of the common people, the reality was that significant changes had taken place during the previous decade. Although there were vast areas of rural landscape, Florida had morphed from a predominantly agricultural state into an urban one. In 1920, 63.5 percent of the population lived on farms or in small towns of fewer than 2,500 persons. By 1930, 51.7 percent of Floridians lived in towns of 2,500 persons or more. Jacksonville, with its 173,000 residents, was the state's largest city, but Miami (172,000) followed closely behind. Tampa, with its population of 108,000, ran a distant third. The other metropolitan areas of the state—Orlando, Tallahassee, Pensacola, St. Petersburg—measured their populations in the lesser thousands. Regardless of locale, the Sunshine State's 1.9 million residents faced a bleak future.

Unemployment, which hit a nationwide high of 25.0 percent in 1932 and averaged 17.3 percent for the remainder of the decade, was even higher in the Sunshine State. With no major industries producing essential goods, Florida's service industries found it difficult to absorb the growing urban population. Some, like Tampa's cigar industry, continued to operate, but even that mainstay of the city's economy experienced layoffs and reduced production. In Ybor City, the Latin community of Tampa, workers' radical support for socialism and the Spanish Republic gave civic leaders concerns about what the future held in such unstable economic times.

More conservative community leaders lent their support to an incipient fascist movement, drawing their ideological models from the orderly and apparently prosperous regimes of Benito Mussolini and, later, Adolph Hitler. Although outnumbered by left-leaning workers, the presence of fascists created a community crisis until the United States entered World War II in 1941. The fear of radical movements from the political left and right continued to haunt traditional business, civic and political leaders in Florida for the entire decade.

Throughout Florida, municipal governments, faced with declining tax bases, found it increasingly difficult to provide even the most rudimentary of services. Government and other public employees frequently found it necessary either to stop working or to agree to being paid with scrip, promissory notes or letters of credit, which they used to pay bills or purchase necessary supplies from local merchants. Still, such crude methods of payment were better than none at all. In Jacksonville, banker Alfred I. du Pont spent thousands of dollars on a public works program that hired unemployed workers to keep the city clean. Few other cities had such wealthy patrons willing to invest in the public weal. Charitable organizations with limited resources offered what they could in the way of relief but quickly found themselves taxed to their monetary limits.

In the rural areas of the state, the Depression exacted an even higher toll. Overproduction of crops like cotton and tobacco had exhausted the soils of central Florida and depressed the national market. Protective tariffs imposed by Congress to protect American farmers produced the opposite effect and closed international markets to American products and goods. Tenant farming and sharecropping, largely based on securing an annual source of credit, came to a halt when few banks were willing to lend money. Some otherwise honest farmers turned to the manufacture of illicit liquor, but even that market dried up when the Volstead Act and the Eighteenth Amendment were repealed in 1933. As the economic situation worsened, Florida farmers relied more and more on living a subsistence existence. Reduced to living off the land, some Floridians fondly remember eating out-of-season venison, turkeys and even deep-fried robins. Tortoises were a particular favorite and were laughingly referred to as "Hoover chickens."

Black Floridians, occupying the bottom rung of the economic ladder, had begun a massive out-migration to northern cities. As early as 1928, more than 2 percent of the state's African American population had left, and this trend increased during the 1930s. With little to no resources of their own, blacks exacerbated the growing unemployment problem in these cities and further depressed job markets. For white Floridians, securing employment during the Depression was difficult, but for African Americans, it was practically impossible. Signs appeared in Florida and other southern states that summed up the plight of blacks succinctly: "No jobs for niggers until every white man has a job." Many whites, realizing the gross inequities that existed in the economy of the Sunshine State, carefully monitored their black neighbors for signs of radical change.

The Jim Crow system, long a staple of southern discrimination, became even more firmly entrenched. In the Sunshine State, the Ku Klux Klan, which had lost membership nationwide following the scandals of the late 1920s, remained strong with a membership base of thirty-three thousand. Although lynchings, which numbered forty-four in the 1920s, dropped to only thirteen during the 1930s, Florida still led the nation in carrying out these criminal acts, one-third of which occurred in urban settings with white, immigrant and African American victims. The Communist Party, which had invaded the South in the 1920s to organize sharecroppers and tenant farmers, and the rise of A. Phillip Randolph—a Crescent City native—in effectively organizing African American porters into a labor union produced a wave of apprehension on the part of southerners. When the Communist Party took an active role in championing the cause of nine black men who were convicted of rape in Scottsboro, Alabama, in 1931, political leaders in all of the southern states were sure that this was the beginning of the radicalization of the African American population. While the influence of the Communist Party eventually came to naught, whites realized that the existing conditions—joblessness, racial discrimination, racial-motivated violence—might fuel a radical uprising of African Americans, and they redoubled their efforts to maintain control. Not since the slave uprisings of the early 1800s had the South experienced such uncertainty in race relations.

Seeking someone to blame for the sudden failure of the American economy, Floridians joined millions of other Americans in listening to the weekly radio broadcasts of Father Charles Coughlin, a Catholic priest based at the Shrine of the Little Flower in Royal Oak, Michigan. Beginning in 1923, Coughlin took to the airwaves to protest social injustice, initially in response to the Ku Klux Klan's burning of crosses on his church's grounds. By 1930, he had claimed a nationwide audience of millions, supported Franklin D. Roosevelt's run for the presidency in 1932 and called the

New Deal "God's work." Gradually, however, he grew disenchanted with Roosevelt and embraced the radical beliefs of the fascists in Germany and Italy. By 1935 and 1936, he was beginning to express radical anti-Semitic ideas and blamed the Depression on "an international clique of Jewish bankers." Despite government measures to stop his broadcasts and to limit the distribution of his newspaper, *Social Justice*, Coughlin found ways to get his message out. He was willing to forgive any extreme policy of the fascists because they were "fighting Bolshevism and the Jewish conspiracy." Following the Japanese attack on Pearl Harbor, Coughlin's bishop stepped in and ordered him to quit broadcasting and writing or face excommunication. He complied and abandoned his campaigns. He remained a priest at Little Flower until 1966. He died in 1979.

Coughlin was not the only person to see sinister forces behind the Depression. In Louisiana, Huey P. Long claimed the governorship in 1928 and a seat in the U.S. Senate in 1932. He appealed to voters with an anti-establishment philosophy that drew on the Populist ideas of William Jennings Bryan. Although initially a supporter of the New Deal, Long broke with Roosevelt in 1933 and formed his own political party, which he hoped would lead to success in the presidential election of 1936. With the slogan "Every Man a King," Long called for the massive redistribution of America's wealth. Many Floridians, accustomed to Populist leaders such as Sidney J. Catts, signed on to the Long effort. His assassination in 1935 ended his challenge to Roosevelt, but the Long political machine would dominate Louisiana politics for the next sixty years.

On January 1, 1934, Americans were offered another solution to their economic woes when Dr. Francis E. Townsend of Long Beach, California, formally announced his plan to create a system whereby every American sixty years of age or older, regardless of his wealth, would receive $200 a month for the duration of his life. The so-called Townsend Plan was to be financed by a flat-rate tax of 2 percent on all business transactions. The only restrictions to be imposed were that the recipients had to agree to spend the entire monthly pension amount in the United States within thirty days of receiving it, recipients had to agree to abandon all future work for wages and recipients had to prove a "past life...free from habitual criminality." Within a year, more than 20 million Americans—including thousands of Floridians—added their names to a petition asking Congress to enact the plan. Although opponents of the plan insisted that it was unworkable because of the high cost, and although it was never enacted, the Townsend

Plan had a positive impact on the creation of the Social Security system. Two million Americans joined Dr. Townsend's Old Age Revolving Pension Club. Townsend continued to be active in the movement to increase retirement pensions until his death in 1960.

The willingness of Americans, particularly those of the lower and middle classes, to embrace movements that called for changes to the prevailing free market system of capitalism was worrisome to the nation's wealthy class. The attempted assassination of President-elect Roosevelt and the killing of Chicago mayor Anton Cermak in Miami by the Italian immigrant Guiseppe Zangara in March 1933 convinced many Americans that the 1930s would be a decade of radical upheavals. Communism, Trotskyism, socialism and anarchism found willing followers, particularly among American intellectuals.

The labor union movement in America gained new prominence. In 1932, Congress approved the Norris-LaGuardia Act, which prohibited federal courts from intervening in strikes by workers organizing in a certain industry. The National Labor Relations Act, passed in 1935, explicitly granted workers the right to organize. Reality, however, was much different. Although laborers might have the legal right to organize, and although courts were prohibited from issuing injunctions, industrialists resorted to private armies to attack labor organizers. Governors frequently brought in the state militia to prevent violence, and generally the militia operated on the site of factory owners. Unions did enjoy some successes, such as gaining the right to organize workers at the General Motors plant in Flint, Michigan, in February 1937. Chrysler Motors also bowed to union demands and allowed its workers to unionize. On the other hand, Henry Ford used gangs of toughs to intimidate and harass labor organizers. In May 1937, for example, his henchmen attacked organizers outside the River Rouge Plant. Although the National Labor Relations Board found Ford Motor Company guilty of violating the rights of workers, Ford managed to stave off unionization for another four years.

Some southern state legislatures hastily enacted "right to work" or "open shop" legislation. Florida, which had few factory workers—with the exception of Ybor City's cigar workers—delayed acting until 1943, when an amendment to the state's constitution was passed to make open shops the standard for industries.

A less organized and less visible disenchantment with capitalism grew among the thousands of farmers and agricultural workers in America. Woodrow Wilson "Woody" Guthrie gave voice to the plight of farmers in his folk songs, while John Steinbeck drew an unforgettable picture of the sufferings they endured and the hopelessness of their condition. Margaret Bourke-White and Erskine Caldwell photographed the realities of life in the rural South and published their findings in *You Have Seen Their Faces*. Marion Post Walcott, Arthur Rothstein, Walker Evans and Russell Lee worked with the Farm Security Administration creating a visual record of the travails of American farm families. Arthur F. Raper also contributed to the literature on the life of farmers with two major books, *Sharecroppers All* (1941) and *Tenants of the Almighty* (1943).

Florida's crime rate, which had exploded during the Roaring Twenties when the number of inmates in the state prison system increased a dramatic 90 percent, continued to rise in the 1930s. Prohibition and the large number of temporary visitors to the state—all bringing money and seeking to live the Florida high life—had produced an amazing increase in the prison population that was not matched until the drug wars and the Mariel boatlift of the 1970s and 1980s. Although the 41 percent increase in the state prison population during the '30s was less than one-half of the previous ten years, it was significant. Urban and rural populations experienced the same rise in crime, brought on by a depressed economy that offered few job opportunities and little in the way of city, county, state or federal aid.

In the Sunshine State, John Dillinger, "Pretty Boy" Floyd, Willie Sutton, Bonnie Parker and Clyde Barrow, notorious bank robbers, were heroes to the rural population, which vicariously identified with the outlaws' attacks on the banking establishments and their reckless disregard for authority. Like Al Capone in the early '30s, some of these bandits took leisurely vacations in Florida, enjoying a respite from their toils and the warm climate. Floridians were not shocked to hear the radio announcement that Arizona Clark "Ma" Barker and her son, Floyd, had been killed in a shootout with law enforcement officers in Lake Weir, in central Florida, on January 16, 1935. It was to be expected.

The administration of Herbert Hoover appeared helpless to bring the economy out of its doldrums. Elected in 1928 because of his quick and efficient response to the problems of post–World War I Europe as the head of the American Relief Administration and his handling of relief agencies in the great Mississippi River flood of 1927, his reputation as the "Great Humanitarian" could not sustain his popularity as the conservative beliefs of his Republican background collided with the demands for government aid. Hoover took credit for the establishment of the Reconstruction Finance

Corporation, which relieved the credit problems of large banking, insurance and industrial firms. While Hoover believed that such policies would create new jobs, stimulate production and increase consumer spending, real benefits did not "trickle down" to the rest of the economy; nor did they end the Depression. Once perceived as a man of action, Hoover was roundly cursed for his inactivity in ending the Depression and unfairly blamed for causing it. Hastily constructed communities of the homeless and unemployed were derisively referred to as "Hoovervilles," and by 1931 little was left of his good reputation.

Floridians joined the forty-five thousand World War I veterans who marched on the nation's capital and settled in a vast shantytown on Anacostia Flats in June 1932. In 1924, Congress passed the Adjusted Service Certificate Act, which granted each veteran $1.00 for each day of domestic service up to $500.00, while veterans who served overseas were granted a

Although Douglas MacArthur was a hero during World War II as he led his troops to reclaim territory from the Japanese, many GIs remembered his attack on the Bonus Army and despised him. *Courtesy of the Camp Blanding Museum.*

payment of $1.25 for each day they spent out of the United States up to a total of $625.00. The payments were to compensate veterans for "wartime suffering" and the loss of income while serving. Veterans were issued certificates that were scheduled to be redeemed in 1945, but because of the Depression, veterans sought to have these certificates honored earlier. Although the veterans had the support of the majority of the members of Congress, President Hoover and his Republican supporters in the Senate opposed immediate redemption of the bonds. Refusing to go home without payment, the veterans waited. On July 28, U.S. attorney general William D. Mitchell ordered the District of Columbia police to evacuate the camp, but after the police shot and killed two veterans who resisted, the police withdrew.

Herbert Hoover ordered the United States Army, under the command of General Douglas MacArthur, to remove the veterans forcibly. With troops from Fort Howard, Maryland, and a force of six battle tanks under the command of Major George S. Patton, MacArthur attacked. At first, the Bonus Marchers thought the army was moving to support them, but after a cavalry charge and the use of adamsite gas (which induces violent vomiting), followed quickly by an infantry attack with fixed bayonets, the veterans scattered. Several veterans were killed, and Hoover called off the attack. MacArthur refused to obey the order to halt and chased the marchers across the river. The Bonus March was over.

The establishment's fear that the marchers were the harbingers of a radical rebellion fueled the confrontation. Franklin D. Roosevelt, who inherited the problem in 1933, attempted to placate veterans by creating twenty-five thousand jobs for them in the Civilian Conservation Corps. When 258 veterans were killed by a hurricane while working on the construction of the Overseas Highway from Miami to Key West in 1935, Congress, over Roosevelt's veto, authorized the payment of bonuses in 1936 in order to avoid more negative publicity and the threat of more extreme action by veterans.

Roosevelt, a New York patrician, promised Americans a "New Deal" in the election of 1932 and swept to an Electoral College landslide. The 444 votes Hoover garnered in 1928 disappeared, and he was reduced to a mere 59. Although few American voters had any idea of what the New Deal would bring, they were ready for change—any change. In Florida, Roosevelt received 74.68 percent of the total votes cast in the election. Not a single county went into the Hoover column.

When FDR took office in March 1933, he immediately called Congress into special session to enact new legislation ranging from the Federal Emergency Relief Administration to providing funds for the unemployed to establishing the Civil Works Administration in order to create jobs. These initial efforts were soon followed by the Works Progress Administration and the Public Works Administration, each focusing on specific segments of the unemployed population and each concentrating on different areas of public works. Following a three-day "banking holiday," which sought to infuse confidence in the banking system and to halt "runs" on banks by giving the banks time to get their affairs in order, Roosevelt promised that no unsound bank would reopen its doors. The Federal Deposit Insurance Corporation, another emergency measure, protected depositor accounts, while the Farm Credit Act provided loans for farmers to purchase seed and equipment and for operations. The National Industrial Recovery Act granted businesses the same guarantees.

Among the most popular New Deal programs was the Emergency Conservation Work Act, which employed 250,000 young, unskilled Americans in jobs that involved reforestation and combating soil erosion. Organized along paramilitary lines and frequently under the command of military officers, the Civilian Conversation Corps (or CCC, as the work units were called) operated camps in all forty-eight states. There were twenty-two camps in Florida, and more than 40,000 young men were put to work in the initial program. At first, southern political leaders wanted to reserve all of the 250,000 jobs for white men, but after Roosevelt threatened to exclude southern states from the program, they relented. Although most CCC camps were segregated, African Americans were included, but in far smaller numbers.

In 1934, the Federal Emergency Relief Administration (FERA), another of the New Deal agencies, undertook the construction of a highway from Miami to Key West, following the general path of Henry Flagler's Florida East Coast Railroad. Three FERA camps were built, and jobs were offered to some of the veterans who participated in the Bonus March. Under the supervision of the Florida Road Department, they set about with a will. The hurricane of 1935 disrupted the project, but in March 1939, the highway opened to the motoring public.

There were numerous other "alphabet" agencies that offered work opportunities or poured federal money into the economy. Among the first relief measures passed by Congress was the Agricultural Adjustment Act, which created the Agricultural Adjustment Administration (AAA) under the aegis of Secretary of Agriculture Henry A. Wallace, a firm believer in government action in economic and social matters, who was as concerned about the rural poor as FDR. Within the administrative framework of the AAA was the Division of Program Planning, which included a Land Policy Section (LPS) that sought to create programs that would upgrade land use. It worked closely with the National Resources Committee (NRC), a privately funded organization with the same goals.

In 1934, after surveying sites in several southern states, the LPS-NRC selected central Florida as a prime area for the creation of a pilot land management program. John Wallace, brother of Secretary Wallace, was among the survey group, and on January 9, 1935, he was named the project manager for what would ultimately become the Withlacoochee Land Use Project. After establishing his headquarters in Brooksville, Wallace and his team of engineers, surveyors, foresters and lawyers began the task of acquiring land for the program, which became part of the Department of Agriculture's Resettlement Administration. Initial plans called for the purchase of 250,000 acres in Pasco, Hernando, Citrus and Sumter Counties in west central Florida, but two congressional budget revisions reduced the amount of money available, so Wallace was able to secure only 113,000 acres.

Within the four counties that constituted the Withlacoochee area, more than 50 percent of the population was on some form of relief, while within the actual project area, the rate was even higher. Of the land purchased for the project, 95 percent was in the process of being foreclosed by state and county authorities for nonpayment of taxes. Federal purchase of the land would provide at least a modicum of financial relief for individuals and regional governments. The proposed project would involve hiring individuals from the local area and would pour thousands of dollars into the local communities in wages. During the first two years of the project's existence, hundreds of men found employment with the program. In December 1935, 166 men were employed, and by March 1936, the monthly figure had risen to 899. One year later, the figure had fallen to an average of 500 a month, but federal employment brought a total of $261,307 in wages into the local economy annually.

One much ballyhooed New Deal program was the Social Security system, designed to provide small monthly incomes to individuals who were too old or infirm to be part of the labor force. The small government stipend, so supporters of the measure argued, would take these people out of the hunt for jobs, thereby making employment more readily available to younger persons with families. In addition, the argument ran, the small stipend would relieve families of much of the burden of caring for elderly members. Although Roosevelt signed the legislation creating the system in 1935, several court cases delayed its implementation. Payroll taxes were first collected in 1937, also the year in which the first lump-sum death benefits were paid to 53,236 beneficiaries. The first reported Social Security payment was to Ernest Ackerman, who retired only one day after Social Security began. Five cents were withheld from his pay during that period, and he received a lump-sum payout of seventeen cents. The first regular monthly payment was issued on January 31, 1940, too late to have an impact on the Depression.

There were occasional bright spots in the otherwise dismal economy of the state. For Tampa's people, the Depression struck hard. The adjusted unemployment rate for white males was 10.8 percent, but that figure almost doubled when individuals involved in emergency government employment—the CCC, WPA and PWA—were counted. For non-whites and women, the rate was even higher. With virtually no manufacturing base for heavy industry, citizens relied heavily on the annual influx of tourists to supplement the local economy. Tampa Shipbuilding and Engineering Company, which had been in operation since February 1917, offered some hope in 1938 when it borrowed $750,000 from the Public Works Administration to fund the construction of a ten-thousand-ton dry dock. The company's objective was to compete for shipbuilding contracts available through the U.S. Maritime Commission and authorized by the Merchant Marine Act of 1936.

Under the leadership of Ernest Kreher, Tampa Shipbuilding secured a PWA loan, constructed a dry dock and, in 1939, was awarded an $8 million contract for the construction of four cargo ships. The excitement created by the contract award was soon dampened when the company announced that after the construction of a single ship, the *Seawitch*, it was in serious financial difficulty and might not be able to fulfill the remaining contracts.

The inefficient management of the company prompted the Maritime Commission and the Reconstruction Finance Corporation, which had assumed the PWA loan, to look around for new owners. In the words of a U.S. Accounting Office report in 1942, "Kreher…and his associates were competent shipbuilders, [but] they were incapable of efficiently managing the company's finances." The heavy demands for ships generated by the war in Europe and the realization that the United

Cloudy Skies in the Sunshine State

The Tampa Shipyard (TASCO) was a major producer of freighters for the federal government during World War II. It employed almost sixteen thousand workers—men and women—at the height of the war. *Courtesy of the Tampa-Hillsborough Library System.*

States might soon be involved made it imperative to find someone new to oversee the administration of the company. Encouraged by the Maritime Commission and the RFC, a local financier, George B. Howell of the Exchange National Bank, purchased the company for $500 and became the sole owner. Along with the contracts for three new ships, Howell also acquired $47,000 in assets and the almost $1 million in liabilities. Under Howell's leadership, TASCO, as the new company was called, worked to fill the contracts with the Maritime Commission. When war came in 1941, the new management was in place and ready to expand to meet the needs of the nation.

By the late 1930s, the Sunshine State had also seen the first of what would become scores of new military installations constructed. Worried about events in Europe and the likelihood of war, the War Department began to build up its training facilities. In 1935, the Navy Department expanded pilot training operations and created a cadet-training program in Pensacola. In 1939, the Navy Department sent a small contingent of thirteen men to an isolated barrier island across the Indian River Lagoon from the small town of Melbourne to build the Banana River Naval Air Station. Hundreds of locals found ready employment with the navy as heavy equipment operators and construction workers.

In north Florida, Camp Foster, the state's National Guard training facility on the shore of the St. Johns River, was turned over to the navy, and a new thirty-thousand-acre site was carved out of rural Clay County. Once again, construction of the new training site—called Camp Blanding in honor of General Albert H. Blanding, the National Guard commander—brought many new jobs and much-needed money to this depressed area. The navy's renovation of Camp Foster and its transformation—along with several outlying bases—into Naval Air Station Jacksonville in 1939–40 pumped additional millions of dollars into the city's economy. Outside the bases, merchants, bar owners, tattoo parlors and "women of the night" experienced a mini boom as sailors and marines poured into the cities and towns.

The New Deal and military construction did not offer a panacea for all the economic woes of Florida or the nation, but the multitude of "make work" agencies slowly decreased the number of unemployed persons. The Great Depression had arrived early in Florida when the land boom collapsed in 1927, and the stock market's crash in 1929 merely added to the state's difficulties. Certainly, when the decade of the 1930s opened, the words of one rural Brevard County resident rang true. "Florida was," he said, "mostly a collection of desperate people with little to enjoy but warm breezes and endless boredom." With the beginning of Roosevelt's administration in 1933, however, there was also hope.

Chapter 2

THE WORLD AT WAR

The 1930s

In a military sense Great Britain and the British Empire are today the spearhead of resistance to world conquest. And they are putting up a fight which will live forever in the story of human gallantry. There is no demand for sending an American expeditionary force outside our own borders. There is no intention by any member of your government to send such a force. You can therefore, nail any talk about sending armies to Europe as deliberate untruth. Our national policy is not directed toward war. Its sole purpose is to keep war away from our country and away from our people.
—*Franklin Delano Roosevelt, December 1940*

The Depression was a major concern of Americans during the 1930s, but it was not their only one. Like most of their neighbors, Floridians watched with apprehension the events that were transpiring in Europe and Asia during the 1930s. The Great War, which had been fought as the "War to End All Wars," was barely a decade in the past. Over 4 million Americans had been called to service in that war; 204,002 were wounded, some grievously, and 53,402 lost their lives. Throughout the 1920s, the United States had played an active role in the various disarmament conferences that sought to limit the ability of countries to make war, and although the United States did not become a member of the League of Nations (the forerunner of today's United Nations), American presidents strongly supported its activities.

Americans were divided in their opinions on the rise of Mussolini's Italy and Hitler's Germany. Some looked at the stability that the fascists managed to impose on the chaotic Italian society and were envious. Similarly, the apparent economic miracles wrought by Hitler in Germany elicited much admiration, and some prominent Americans, such as Charles A. Lindbergh, were vocal in their support of the "New" Germany. The Italian invasion of Ethiopia in April 1935 and the joint German-Italian support of Generalissimo Francisco Franco's revolt against the Spanish Republic in 1936 impressed some Americans with the strength inherent in fascism. The involvement of the Soviet Union on the side of the Republic presaged the epic struggles that swamped Europe in the early 1940s.

In 1933, Germany withdrew from the League of Nations. It renounced the Treaty of Versailles in 1935 and, in 1936, abandoned all of its international agreements. Although the German military had been quietly expanding its forces since the early 1930s, in 1935 Hitler announced that the army, which had been limited to a small force of 100,000 soldiers, would immediately expand its ranks to 500,000 equipped with the latest weapons. The rush to reconstitute and rearm the German military provided the impetus that country needed to overcome the decade-long depression that had seen the mark, the basic unit of German currency, suffer from hyperinflation. (For example, in 1923, one pound of bread cost 3 billion marks, one pound of meat cost 36 billion marks and a single glass of beer cost 4 billion marks.) Increasing the size of the army through conscription and building an entirely new navy and air force meant that hundreds of thousands of Germans could find gainful employment. Industrial concerns, like Krupp, Messerschmitt and I.G. Farben, began to expand their facilities to meet the demand for new weapons and supplies. By 1935, just two years after taking power, Hitler could rightly claim that he had revived Germany.

In March 1936, despite the opposition of the German officer corps, Hitler decided to remilitarize the Ruhr Valley, Germany's industrial heartland, which formally ended the terms imposed by the victorious Allies at the end of World War I. In March 1938, he sent the German army into neighboring Austria to oversee a forced union (*anschluss*) of that country with Germany. Not satisfied, he immediately began a campaign to annex the Sudetenland, a German-speaking area of Czechoslovakia, an adjoining country that had been created by the Treaty of Versailles in 1919. Threatening to go to war to protect Germans in the area, a hastily convened conference in Munich awarded him the territory over the protests of the Czech government in

September 1938. In March 1939, Hitler invaded and annexed the remainder of the Czech Republic.

In 1937, Mussolini took Italy out of the League of Nations following the outcry against its use of poison gas in Ethiopia, support of Franco in Spain and the imposition of economic sanctions by member states of the league. Following Hitler's lead, Mussolini sent Italian forces into Albania in April 1939 and claimed it as part of the newly created Italian empire. One month later, the two fascist leaders cemented an alliance—the so-called Pact of Steel. With the failure of other countries to meet force with force, Hitler concluded that democracy was dying and soon would be dead.

There were some Americans who agreed with Hitler's philosophy, and in the early 1930s, the German-American Bund, a neo-Nazi organization, was created in New York. For the rest of the decade, the members of this group echoed the racist propaganda of the German Nazi party. In 1936, Fritz Julius Kuhn, the American "Fuehrer," led a delegation of Americans to Germany. Although Hitler avoided a sit-down meeting with Kuhn and largely ignored his presence in Germany, Kuhn reported to his American supporters that he had received the blessings of Hitler. In February 1939, the Bund held a rally at Madison Square Gardens that was attended by more than twenty thousand persons. It was the high-water mark of the Nazi movement in the United States.

Across the Pacific Ocean, the military-controlled government of Japan, although nominally a monarchy, launched an attack on Manchuria in September 1931, following the so-called Mukden Incident, followed closely by continued skirmishes with the army of Chiang Kai Shek's Nationalist Republic of China. *Time* and *Life* magazines, along with the country's newspapers, provided Americans with a blow-by-blow account of the invasion. Not content with just Manchuria, the Japanese military began to manufacture a series of "incidents" with China. On July 7, 1937, a major, but undeclared, war erupted after a confrontation at the Marco Polo Bridge near Beijing (Peking). In rapid succession, the Japanese attacked other Chinese cities, pitting their well-trained and modern-equipped army against the peasant army of the Nationalists. The war in China would continue until 1945.

In 1937, American relations with Japan were strained when Japanese airplanes deliberately sank an American gunboat, the *Panay*, in the Yangtze River. Although Japan claimed that the incident was an accident, promptly apologized, paid more than $2 million in restitution and recalled the officers responsible for the attack, it heightened the tensions between the two nations. In 1940, following Japan's invasion of Indochina, the United States imposed an embargo on the sale of scrap metals to that nation. In June 1941, the United States also imposed a total embargo on the sale of American oil to the Japanese, who had no available sources; oil was essential for the continued operations of their armed forces. War between the two powers appeared to be inevitable.

In the United States, political leaders were divided over the proper course the nation should take in regard to the European and Asian events. Some, such as Senator Burton K. Wheeler, Senator William E. Borah, Senator Gerald P. Nye and Senator David I. Walsh, were active in pushing the idea of isolationism and argued that the United States had nothing to gain by choosing sides in any European dispute. They were joined by many other prominent Americans, including Charles A. Lindbergh, in speaking out against American involvement in any foreign argument.

Between 1934 and 1936, Senator Nye headed the Special Committee on Investigation of the Munitions Industry, which concluded that American arms manufacturers and bankers who profited from the sales of munitions and from high interest loans to warring countries had brought about America's entry into World War I. Although simplistic in its conclusions, isolationists welcomed the Nye Committee report. Certainly, most Americans agreed that European involvement had to be avoided at all costs, and they likewise advocated noninvolvement in Japan's conquests in China. The United States had too many problems at home to solve. On August 31, 1935, Congress passed the first Neutrality Act, which prohibited the exportation of munitions to countries at war. Although Roosevelt opposed the act, he reluctantly signed it in the face of public support for the measure. When Congress renewed the act in February 1936, he once again went along with it, although it was expanded to prohibit making loans to any belligerent power. The third Neutrality Act, passed in 1937 in the wake of the Spanish Civil War, allowed for warring countries to purchase materiel, except for arms, from U.S. suppliers on a "cash and carry" basis. In response to Germany's occupation of Czechoslovakia in March 1939 and its invasion of Poland in September of that year, Congress passed a final Neutrality Act that did allow for the sale of arms, but strictly on a cash basis. American ships were prohibited from entering the ports of warring nations and combat zones.

Although Roosevelt was handicapped in his dealings with the European countries, he remained convinced that the United States would eventually be drawn into a large-scale war. To this end, he used the power of executive orders to begin preparations for this eventuality. In 1936, he issued an order that prohibited the use of steel in nonessential building projects, reserving this valuable commodity for shipyards. At his insistence, the War Department surveyed existing military facilities, airports and potential sites for new training camps. Military planners, aware of the tremendous technological changes in the way wars were fought and the obsolescence of American equipment, issued requests for the development and production of new airplanes, tanks and vehicles. Although the full-scale production of the new equipment was not implemented immediately, by 1937 and 1938, the design and testing of much of the equipment later used in World War II had been done.

Roosevelt also encouraged the military to expand its training of regular and National Guard units through annual war games. In 1935, the navy instituted its air cadet program at Naval Air Station Pensacola, and soon the number of navy, marine and Coast Guard cadets exceeded the capacity of the facility. Two additional bases were established to accommodate the

The bombers for Jimmy Doolittle's raid on Japan rest on the deck of the carrier USS *Hornet* as the task force makes its way to the Sea of Japan in 1942. *Courtesy of the Eglin Air Force Museum.*

MacDill Army Air Field in Tampa was established originally to fly antisubmarine patrols in the Gulf of Mexico, but it soon became a major training base for American bomber pilots. MacDill is still an active military base today and is home to United States Central Command and United States Special Operations Command. *Courtesy of the Anthony Pizzo Collection, University of South Florida Special Collections.*

overflow—one in Corpus Christi, Texas, and the other in Jacksonville, Florida. The Naval Expansion Act of 1939 further authorized the construction of new facilities, and Florida again reaped benefits. In 1939, the navy began construction of the Banana River Naval Air Station in Brevard County, and the base was commissioned in October 1940, a full year before the United States entered the war. Within a year, the base was ready to receive the first complement of sailors and aviators. Hundreds of unemployed locals found work building the new base. Construction purchases also poured hundreds of thousands of dollars into the local economy as merchants and suppliers were called upon to provision the growing number of sailors.

The navy was not the only service interested in establishing bases in the Sunshine State. In the 1930s, an active group of citizens sought to interest the Army Air Corps in expanding the civilian airport in Valparaiso into an operational base. With a grant from the Federal Emergency Relief Administration, the airport was expanded and essential buildings constructed in March 1935. In June of that year, the facility was turned over to the army and was designated the Valparaiso Bombing and Gunnery Base. On August 4, 1937, the base was renamed Eglin Field in honor of Lieutenant Colonel Frederick I. Eglin, an army aviator who had been killed in a plane crash in January 1937. By 1940, more than one thousand CCC workers were engaged in enlarging the base and constructing barracks for service personnel, housing for workers and hangars and maintenance facilities for aircraft. Eglin's importance to the war effort would lead to further expansion.

In 1939, the Army Air Corps began construction on a new facility on the south end of Interbay Peninsula within the city limits of Tampa. Although originally built as a base for fighter and antisubmarine aircraft, MacDill Field surrendered these operations to the navy and became a major training base for bomber pilots after America's entry into the war. To the south in Arcadia, citizens tried to interest the military in reopening Carlstrom Field, a World War I training base that had been closed in 1926. They were unsuccessful until March 1941, when Riddle Aeronautical Institute entered into a contract with the federal government to train pilots for the British Royal Air Force (RAF). Since the United States was technically neutral in the European war, training was handled by the Riddle Institute, a private educational institution. In August 1941, the first class of new British pilots graduated and was sent back to Great Britain to fly for the RAF. After Pearl Harbor, the army took control of the base and continued to use it for training purposes.

Tallahassee officials, acting through the office of Democratic senator Claude Pepper, persuaded army officials to convert the city's airport, Dale Mabry Field, into a training base. It opened in May 1941. In the center of the state, Hendricks Field, a training base for B-17 Flying Fortress crews, opened in 1940 in Sebring. In Lakeland, Drane Field opened in 1940 as an auxiliary field for bomber crews stationed at MacDill Field in Tampa. In 1941, the U.S. Army Air Force (USAAF) also opened a combat training base for fighter pilots in Punta Gorda in Charlotte County. In early 1941, the USAAF also took control of Morrison Field in Palm Beach. Elsewhere around the Sunshine State, civic and business leaders led movements to secure federal assistance for building new airports. Although the United States was still technically a neutral nation, few people believed that it could avoid war in Europe forever, and established municipal airports would

Hendricks Army Air Field, located in Sebring, was a major training base for pilots of the B-17 bomber, the workhorse of the Allied bombing campaign against Germany. *Courtesy of the Sebring Historical Society.*

certainly bring the military in to take them over. The money spent on converting these facilities into military bases, coupled with the number of service personnel with money to spend, could make or break the economy of any small Florida town.

The Roosevelt administration, disturbed by the inability of American shipyards to compete with foreign yards and aware that the clouds of war gathering in Europe and Asia might soon cover the United States, prevailed upon Congress to enact the Merchant Marine Act. American shipyards, which had constructed only two dry cargo vessels between 1922 and 1935, were offered "no lose" contracts for the construction of ten ships a year for ten years. In addition, the Public Works Administration made low interest loans available to renovate existing yards. In 1939, the Tampa Shipbuilding and Engineering Company was awarded an $8 million contract for the construction of four cargo ships. About two thousand new jobs were created, and for the city's sixty-four hundred unemployed males, the company's success in securing the contracts seemed like the answer to their prayers. The original owners of the company proved incompetent, and by 1940, the company was under new management and had been renamed TASCO. Within a year, the new company employed sixteen thousand workers, and a second shipyard, Hooker's Point, was under construction.

War in Europe became a reality when Germany invaded Poland on September 1, 1939. Throughout the remainder of 1939 and all of 1940, President Roosevelt skirted the technicalities of the Neutrality Acts by providing the countries fighting Hitler with military equipment through a "cash and carry" arrangement. After the fall of France in June 1940, Great Britain faced the Germans alone. When the British could no longer afford to pay for war materiel, the United States allowed them to purchase critically needed supplies on credit. In September 1940, Roosevelt worked out the "Destroyers for Bases" deal that allowed Great Britain to take possession of fifty American World War I destroyers in exchange for the right to build American military bases in Canada and in British possessions in the Caribbean. In addition, the United States Navy undertook the task of escorting supply convoys across the Atlantic.

Although President Roosevelt promised to keep American youths out of the war, he urged congressional leaders to help him prepare for the eventuality that the United States could not avoid it. In September 1940, Congress approved the Selective Service Act, which required all males between the ages of twenty-one and thirty-five to register for military service.

This was the first peacetime draft in American history, and 900,000 young men were called up for a tour of twelve months. In August 1941, the term of service was extended past one year, much to the chagrin of the draftees. Nevertheless, when the Japanese attacked Pearl Harbor on December 7, 1941, the foundations for a modern military were in place.

Some economic historians have argued that the Great Depression did not end until the United States entered World War II. Nationwide, as production of war materiel grew and the military expanded its forces through the draft, unemployment fell rapidly—from 17.2 percent in 1939 to 4.7 percent in 1942 to an amazing 1.2 percent in 1944. By 1942, the task employers were facing was finding enough workers for all the jobs that needed doing. Civilian employment rose from 45.8 million in 1939 to 54 million in 1944, even as the armed forces expanded from 300,000 to 11.5 million personnel during the same period. Floridians, who had started reaping the benefits of the American buildup of bases and defense industries before 1941, would benefit even more when the United States entered the war.

Chapter 3

Pearl Harbor Mobilizes the Florida Homefront

The major objectives of a sound manpower policy are: First, to select and train men of the highest fighting efficiency needed for our armed forces in the achievement of victory over our enemies in combat...Second, to man our war industries and farms with the workers needed to produce the arms and munitions and food required by ourselves and by our fighting allies to win this war...In order to do this, we shall be compelled to stop workers from moving from one war job to another as a matter of personal preference; to stop employers from stealing labor from each other; to use older men, and handicapped people, and more women, and even grown boys and girls, wherever possible and reasonable, to replace men of military age and fitness; to train new personnel for essential war work; and to stop the wastage of labor in all non-essential activities...In some communities, employers dislike to employ women. In others they are reluctant to hire Negroes. In still others, older men are not wanted. We can no longer afford to indulge such prejudices or practices.
—Franklin Delano Roosevelt, October 1942

O ver the next four years, more than 250,000 Floridians—male and female—would serve in the armed forces of the United States. An additional 300,000 volunteered for duty in one of the many civilian agencies that supported the war effort. From coastal submarine watches in lonely towers on vacant beaches to serving on draft boards, from operating USO halls to becoming air raid marshals and everything in between, Florida civilians willingly joined the fight. Within a few months, they, like other Americans, organized drives to save grease (for munitions), scrap metal of all kinds, rubber to be recycled for tires and other useful materials such as rags and paper. By the spring of 1942, every man, woman and child in the state had been issued a "ration" book, filled with coupons that limited the amounts of meat, sugar, canned goods and other foodstuffs that could be purchased each week. Victory gardens were planted to produce needed vegetables, while meatless days—one day a week—became common for every family. Farmers suddenly became very popular as foodstuffs became more difficult to buy, while butchers who "saved something" for their longtime customers enjoyed just as much popularity. By November 1943, rationed items included bicycles, fuel oil, coffee, stoves, shoes, meat, lard, shortening and oils, cheese, butter, margarine, processed foods, dried fruits, canned milk, firewood and coal, jams, jellies and fruit butter.

Scrap metal of various kinds was collected in drives throughout the state. This photograph shows the results of an aluminum collection drive in Casselberry. The aluminum collected was used in the manufacture of aircraft. *Courtesy of the Orange County Regional History Center.*

The federal Office of Price Administration (OPA) also set limits on the number of gallons of gasoline automobile owners could buy each week. Initially aimed at discouraging pleasure, or recreational, driving, the OPA soon extended its limitations on motoring to include all nonessential driving. Automobile owners soon found themselves eligible to buy only three or four gallons per week. Rationing also applied to the purchase of tires, batteries and other replacement parts. Although gas station owners found ways to supply favored customers, some car owners simply parked their vehicles "for the duration" and took to public transportation, selling or giving their ration coupons to others. Officials with the OPA closely monitored the price of gasoline and were equally as diligent policing the claims of workers in carpools for extra gas and tire rations. Violators were charged, prosecuted and punished. The OPA also closely monitored the practices of local

Gasoline, food, automobile parts, tires, meat and numerous other consumer items were rationed during the war years. Citizens carried ration cards and presented them when they purchased restricted goods. A burgeoning black market grew up in towns and cities where citizens could buy rationed items illegally. *Courtesy of the Beaches Historical Society, Jacksonville Beach.*

merchants, and hoarders and speculators were quickly dealt with. A thriving black market soon appeared, however, largely run by the same individuals who had supplied bootleg liquor during Prohibition.

Even the allocation of housing and the amount that could be charged for rent came under the control of various government agencies. Price controls were essential, particularly in urban areas where large numbers of laborers were brought in to work in war industries. As industries expanded their labor forces, workers found it difficult to find accommodations for themselves and their families. Patriotic appeals were frequently made in the newspapers asking homeowners to rent every available apartment or room to house these new arrivals. To ensure that workers were not being gouged by greedy property owners, the Office of Rent Control (ORC) periodically published lists of acceptable rents established by federal regulations, and just as periodically, the ORC sent inspectors into the field to ensure that no gouging was taking place.

Although the families of workers were encouraged to stay home, many accompanied them to the factory towns. Companies often erected "villages" for their workers and their families, usually temporary shelters that sometimes lacked even the basics of running water and sewers. Showers, latrines and kitchens, shared in common, provided essentials, but living in these workers' villages was much like camping out. In Tampa, for example, city leaders, led by Mayor Robert E. Lee Chauncey, quickly took other steps to resolve the problem. The city council voted to lease twelve acres of the Municipal Trailer Park to serve as a park for four hundred two- and three-bedroom trailers for workers and their families. Rather primitive, the trailers had no bathrooms or laundry facilities, and occupants were forced to use a communal building for these purposes. Despite the critical shortage of housing and the relatively low rent (twenty-eight dollars a month for a two-bedroom unit and thirty-two dollars for a three-bedroom unit), the trailer park proved unpopular and never operated at full capacity. Other plans were suggested, including one that called for cities to turn vacant factory buildings into apartments. Although the idea seemed worthwhile, it was quickly abandoned because the cost of renovation was greater than that of new construction.

Similar measures were taken by every town and city in Florida, but adequate housing for workers, their families and the million or so trainees who came to Florida during the war continued to be a constant concern for government officials throughout the war. Companies often worked with the federal government to find different solutions. For workers at the new

Hooker's Point shipyard in Tampa, considered an essential industry, the Maritime Commission constructed six hundred housing units adjacent to the yard. The project, known as Maritime Homes, represented a considerable improvement over the trailers. Each unit included its own bathroom, hot water heater and refrigerator. The project also included a grocery store, beauty shop, barbershop and theatre. Restricted to McCloskey workers, the rental prices were only slightly higher than those charged for municipal trailers.

African Americans found it very difficult to find satisfactory housing. The Jim Crow system of segregation that made up the essence of southern society before the war continued during and after it. Still, minor gains were made. Blacks in Tampa suffered from the housing shortage, but this shortage was alleviated somewhat when the city government and the federal Public Housing Authority decided in 1943 to spend $2.3 million to construct five hundred low cost concrete block homes. Justified as a war emergency measure to provide housing for essential shipyard workers, the project was located "in the heart of the largest Negro section in Tampa, and [was]...well served by electricity, water, transportation and Negro schools." The original plans were modified and the number of units reduced when one Tampa council member "asked that three of the big apartment buildings that would have come within five hundred feet of Ponce de Leon courts, [a] white development, be eliminated." Even the desperate need for emergency housing was not a sufficient cause to ease the rigors of segregation.

Elsewhere, hotels and resorts that had operated at reduced levels found a ready market for rooms that had been unoccupied or occupied occasionally during the 1930s. The smaller hotels were quickly filled by workers, while the larger hotels were commandeered by the military and put to use as training schools, hospitals and barracks. In Miami and Miami Beach, four hundred hotels were taken over by the army and navy, which paid owners twenty dollars per month per serviceman housed in them. Larger hotels, like the Biltmore and the Nautilus, were converted into hospitals. Elaborate recreational facilities, which once drew thousands of well-heeled tourists, were converted to drill fields or restricted to military use. One-fourth of the Army Air Force officers, including such luminaries as Clark Gable, and about one-fifth of its enlisted men got their first training on Miami Beach. Irving Rubin, a resident of Miami and later a B-25 pilot, attended officer candidate school in one of the hotels, just a few miles from his home. "It was a little embarrassing," he said, "because my mother and the rest of my family would come to see me every weekend."

D. C. 137—Truck Convoy, Miami Beach, Fla.
Army Air Forces Technical Training Command

Above: Miami Beach, long a tourist mecca, was taken over by the military, and the luxury hotels were used as barracks and training centers for army and navy personnel. *Courtesy of the Jack Rabun Postcard Collection.*

Left: Irving "Irv" Rubin, a native of Miami, went through the officers' training program on Miami Beach. He was one of four siblings who served in the war. *Courtesy of the Florida Historical Society.*

Pearl Harbor Mobilizes the Florida Homefront

Officer candidates do physical training on Miami Beach while wearing hot rubber gas masks. This became a common daily sight in this one-time "hub of high society" in south Florida. *Courtesy of the Florida State Photographic Archives.*

The same pattern was repeated in other parts of the Sunshine State. The Ponce de Leon Hotel in St. Augustine was converted into a Coast Guard indoctrination center, while the Hollywood Beach Hotel housed a similar school for the navy. In Daytona Beach, the Women's Army Auxiliary Corps received training in the large hotels on the beach. In 1942, the army bought the famous Don Cesar Hotel on St. Petersburg Beach for $450,000 and converted it to hospital use. At the Belleview Biltmore in Clearwater, student pilots and officers from MacDill Army Air Force Base in Tampa occupied the rooms that once had been the winter homes of the very wealthy. In order to make this facility safer, elaborate wooden decorations were removed, and an ugly fire suppression system was installed. The championship golf course designed by Donald J. Ross was used as a parade field and allowed to fall into disrepair.

Interestingly, the number of tourists coming to the Sunshine State during the war years was substantially more than the number who came the previous decade. Although the military claimed the largest resorts and hotels, the

The Belleview Biltmore Hotel, Henry Plant's luxury hotel constructed in the 1890s, became quarters for officers from MacDill AAF during the war. Much of the original decorative woodwork in the hotel was removed as a fire safety measure. *Courtesy of the Richard Moorhead Collection.*

Graduating Class — Officers Candidates, A.A.F.T.T.C., Miami Beach, Florida

The graduating class of the Army Air Force Officers' Training School in Miami Beach assembles for a final inspection on the polo fields at a Miami Beach hotel. *Courtesy of the Jack Rabun Postcard Collection.*

Pearl Harbor Mobilizes the Florida Homefront

Florida Chamber of Commerce encouraged tourists to come to the state and take advantage of the 328,934 hotel rooms not being used by the services. Operators were able to ask for and receive full price for their rooms. By the end of 1943, hotel owners had petitioned the federal government to return the commandeered hotels and to relocate training facilities elsewhere. The Office of Price Administration and the Office of Rent Control could do little to prevent hotel operators from getting paid additional money "under the table" for vacancies, nor could they control the black market that filled the demands of tourists for rationed goods. Gambling, long a staple of Sunshine State tourism, returned. During the 1943–44 "season," the Hialeah Racetrack reported taking in more than $600,000 a day in bets, while the state's dog tracks claimed more than $100,000 a night in wagers. Miami, like most big cities, was reviled in the nation's press as an example of "war profiteering and war dodging."

Money, which had been so scarce just a year or so earlier, began to pour into the Sunshine State. The construction of new shipyards and the modernization of others meant that millions of construction dollars were added to the economy. Three counties—Hillsborough, Duval and Bay—accounted for almost half of the federal contracts for war production. In Tampa, Philadelphia businessman Matthew H. McCloskey spent $30 million to build a new shipyard at Hooker's Point, while local banker George B. Howell spent additional millions to upgrade the facilities at the Tampa Shipbuilding Company yard. In Panama City, the J.A. Jones Construction Company pumped more millions into the state's economy when it built the Wainwright Yard. In two years, the Wainwright Yard fielded a labor force of 13,500 workers and constantly sought to expand these numbers even more. In Fort Lauderdale, the Dooley's Basin and Dry Dock Company upgraded its construction facilities so that it could fulfill contracts to build subchasers and rescue boats. In Jacksonville, the Gibbs Gas Engine Company, long a fixture in the community, expanded its operations and became a major builder of tugs, lighters and minesweepers. Tampa Marine, which had been building boats for the Tampa-based banana fleet, changed gears and began to produce small tugs and minesweepers for the army and navy. At Beresford, near DeLand, the American Machinery Company built a boatyard to produce tugs and barges for the army. In Pensacola, the home of the navy's flight training, the Pensacola Shipyard and Engineering Company of Bayou Chico—later Smith's Shipyard—employed 7,000 workers in 1942 to build tugs. The United States Maritime Commission invested $17 million in the St. John's River Shipbuilding Company, operated by the Merrill-Stevens

Company, to build six ways for the construction of EC2-S-C1 Liberty ships. In Miami, the Miami Shipbuilding Company contracted with the Russian and Australian navies to build patrol craft and crash boats, in addition to almost five hundred crash boats for the United States Navy.

The combined labor requirements for all Jacksonville shipyards exceeded thirty-five thousand men and women. Most of these workers came from the rural areas of north Florida and Georgia, but as the war went forward, the draft made finding suitable workers more and more difficult. Like their counterparts in Tampa and Panama City, Jacksonville shipyards scoured the countryside of surrounding states looking for workers. Chronic labor shortages affected all industries in the Sunshine State. Large companies, such as Tampa Shipbuilding (TASCO) and Hooker's Point Shipyard, sent recruiters throughout the South to find workers to fill vacant jobs. TASCO needed a minimum of sixteen thousand workers, while Hooker's Point had a minimum requirement of six thousand. The expansion of a third shipbuilding facility, Tampa Marine Company, also increased the demand for workers. Despite the high rate of unemployment in 1940,

The Wainwright Yard in Panama City, like yards in Tampa and Jacksonville, produced critically needed Victory ships to transport men and supplies to theatres of operation in North Africa, Europe and the Pacific. *Courtesy of the Bay County Public Library.*

Small army tugs were produced at the Beresford Shipyard in DeLand. Small yards, such as the Beresford facility, produced endless quantities of small lighters, tugs and other watercraft that did not require complicated engineering or manufacturing processes. *Courtesy of the Orange County Regional Historical Center.*

Tampa could not supply the labor needs of these facilities, and company officials instituted a statewide recruitment program. When these efforts did not produce enough workers, the campaign was expanded into a nationwide effort.

The campaign to attract workers was never totally effective, and the Tampa shipyards, as well as other industries, attempted to offset the lack of workers by extending the workweek from forty to forty-eight hours. Wages were constantly increased, and appeals were made to operators of nonessential industries to release workers for war industries. Thomas M. Woodward, a member of the U.S. Maritime Commission, noted the importance of women in the labor force on an inspection of the Tampa yards. Citing a need for thirty thousand additional workers in yards along the Gulf of Mexico, Woodward offered the observation that "women seem to be the answer, the only one, to the problem." Women by the thousands took on the roles of

"I've found the job where I fit best!"

FIND YOUR WAR JOB
In Industry – Agriculture – Business

Women were encouraged to join the labor force as men were drafted into the military. Long before Rosie the Riveter became a popular icon, female workers were performing a variety of jobs from welding to assembling aircraft. *Courtesy of the Florida Photographic Archives.*

Small manufacturing concerns, like the American Machinery Company in Casselberry, turned to manufacturing a wide range of crucial war materiel, such as bomb casings. *Courtesy of the Orange County Regional History Center.*

Rosie the Riveter and Wanda the Welder. As the demand for soldiers grew, female workers became more and more essential.

Older males found work in shipyards as well. In Tampa, TASCO actively sought older men with metalworking skills and brought them into its yard. The oldest worker employed by the company was seventy-seven years old in 1943. J.M. Hutchins entered the blacksmithing trade in 1908, worked in the Mobile and Pensacola shipyards during World War I and, in 1942, worked a full shift at TASCO. Others who were advanced in age joined Hutchins: W.M. Lovelace, seventy-five years old; R.F. Roberts, sixty-six years old; and E.L. Broadway, also sixty-six. The special skills these men possessed were critical to the production of steel ships, and they were considered desirable workers. "They're men who were doing this kind of work before many of us were born," said Carl Froehiking, the shop supervisor. "That many years of experience is something that can't be replaced by any other kind of training. Besides, in times like these, we need all the men we can get to keep the iron hot."

Shipyards were not the only businesses that needed workers. In Casselberry, outside Orlando, the American Machinery Company erected factories to produce bombs and parachutes. In Fort Lauderdale, the H.A.K. Corporation produced artillery shells, while the Gate City Sash and Door Company built awning windows that were distributed around the globe to American military bases. Elsewhere in the city, the Rex Bassett Plant produced two-way radios and the Goodwin Awning Company filled contracts for "pup" tents. Around the state, small factories employed men and women to produce war materiel, but its overall manufacturing output was small when compared to the output of older, industrialized states. Still, Floridians contributed to the success of the American industrial juggernaut. Construction companies, building bases, airports, housing and special projects, also faced constant shortages of workers.

Citrus production, vegetable farming, cattle ranching and fishing in the Sunshine State accounted for its greatest contributions to the war effort. In 1942, the federal government requisitioned the entire output of canned and processed citrus fruits for use by the American military and its allies. The demand for Florida citrus was so great that growers had difficulty meeting the demands. Seasonal and migrant workers, traditionally the mainstay of the industry, were in scarce supply as most of them abandoned the groves for better-paying jobs in war industries. Government authorities at the state and national levels instituted an emergency labor program that recruited workers from the Bahamas, Jamaica and Barbados for work in the groves. In

Like meat carcasses in a packinghouse, bomb casings were hung on revolving racks and inspected for flaws. These casings were sent to arsenals to be packed with explosives and then shipped to bases around the world for use against Axis targets. *Courtesy of the Orange County Regional History Center.*

addition, women and high school students were employed to round out the labor force. After 1943, German and Italian prisoners of war were dispatched from Camp Blanding and Aliceville, Alabama, to camps in Winter Haven, Clewiston, Leesburg, Dade City and Marianna to work in the citrus groves.

Truck farmers also utilized foreign workers and prisoners of war to harvest vegetables and peanuts. The same was true of sugarcane producers, who also experienced a scarcity of laborers. Occasionally, military personnel were recruited to work during their off time. In 1943, some seven hundred men from the Buckingham Army Airfield became temporary agricultural workers when a local potato crop was threatened. To further assist farmers, the Department of Agriculture created Farm Labor Supply Centers, which served as collection points for workers who were then sent where needed.

The desperate need for workers moved local governments to take drastic actions. Throughout the state, city officials enacted ordinances to prohibit

Women in a Casselberry factory produce parachutes for use by Allied troops. Once again, women were used as workers. Not only did they prove capable, but they were also essential in replacing men who were drafted or enlisted in the military. *Courtesy of the Orange County Regional History Center.*

"loafing and idling" on city streets. On November 20, 1942, the *St. Petersburg Times* published an Associated Press story that detailed some of the actions taken. J.C. Stone, the police chief in Orlando, reported, "The time has come to clean Orlando of its loitering and idle men who are contributing less than nothing to the war effort." Lakeland officials ordered the city's police force to "check regularly on jook [juke] joints and arrest any men found idling there who cannot show they are gainfully employed on a regular basis." The same held true in Gainesville, Fort Pierce, Sanford, St. Petersburg, Tarpon Springs and elsewhere. So great was the need for workers that little thought was given to the possibility that such arrests violated the individual's constitutional rights. It was, after all, wartime, and everyone had a duty to support the war effort.

During the war years, Florida was abuzz with activity on a variety of fronts. The more than two hundred military bases demanded infrastructure development, and the state embarked on a massive road-building program. From 1940 until 1944, the state added 1,560 miles of paved highways at a cost of more than $44 million. By the end of the war in 1945, Florida could claim more than 8,000 miles of paved roads. Like other industries, road construction demanded laborers and exacerbated the chronic shortage that the state faced.

On September 26, 1943, the Humble Oil Company brought in the state's first commercially viable oil well in the Sunniland Field in northern Collier County and claimed the $50,000 prize offered by the state. By 1945, there were eleven wells in the field, which added about 500,000 barrels to the nation's supply each year. With Humble Oil's success in Collier County, wildcatters began to explore other areas for new fields. Once again, laborers working in speculative oil exploration were not available for work in other industries.

Virtually every segment of Florida's population served in some capacity. Some 350,000 citizens volunteered to fill jobs left vacant by the draft or war industries. The Florida Defense Council, which was made up of 137 local and county councils, placed these volunteers as air raid wardens, nurses' aides, auxiliary firemen and policemen and aircraft spotters. Along the coasts, private citizens volunteered the use of their boats as part of the Coastal Picket Patrol, which kept watch for submarine activities. The Civilian Air Patrol, a group of small private aircraft owners organized in March 1942, flew aerial observation missions along the coast looking for signs of submarine activity. Schoolchildren participated in various drives to collect cooking grease, scrap metal and other items that could be used in the production of war materiel.

In every town and village in the Sunshine State, citizens bought bonds to help fund the war effort. Local civic leaders proudly erected large billboards to display the amounts of money raised during successive bond campaigns. Celebrities toured the nation encouraging citizens to invest their savings in war bonds, and rallies of all sizes were held to generate patriotic fervor for buying bonds. The U.S. military employed hundreds of men and women—fighter aces, medal winners, wounded and recuperating veterans, choral groups, bands, movie stars—in bond drives. Soldiers, sailors, marines and members of all branches of the service were encouraged to put a portion of their pay into bonds. War industries competed with one another to see which could raise the most money, and the federal government was quick to recognize their efforts.

Above: Bond drives were held periodically to encourage members of the armed services and the civilian population to spend their savings to purchase bonds, which were used to fund the war effort. *Courtesy of the Florida Photographic Archives.*

Right: An enlisted navy man delivers war bonds to the WAVE personnel at the Melbourne Naval Air Station. Service units were assigned quotas, and military officers encouraged those serving under them to meet or exceed these quotas. *Courtesy of the Brevard County Historical Commission.*

Individual citizens were encouraged to take their savings out of banks and to purchase war bonds. Children saved money in their piggy banks and got their pictures in newspapers when they used their savings for bond purchases. Even if an individual could not qualify for military service or work in a war industry, buying a bond allowed him to feel like he was "doing his part" to win the war.

Men, women, the aged, the young, the infirm and everyone in between contributed in some way to ensure that the United States would not fail. America had been attacked, and now the attackers would face the full fury of a united American population. Like their fellow citizens in other states, Floridians rose to meet the challenges created by the war. Within months of the Pearl Harbor attack, Florida's homefront was mobilized.

Chapter 4

WAR COMES TO FLORIDA

U-boats and Alien Spies

Heading south from Jax Beach after successful attack on tanker; nearing St. Augustine...
Lucky night! Another tanker spotted heading north only a few hundred yards from the
coast. Released the last of our eels; direct hit! We approached to finish the task. We were
close enough, and the fires were bright enough, to read the name of the ship as we passed
in front of it. the SS GulfAmerica. Rumor has it that this is the newest vessel in the
Gulf Oil fleet, carrying over 90,000 tons of fuel oil. It won't be going to New York as
planned, I'm afraid...We approached from the coastward side and opened fire with our
deck machine gun. The crew was abandoning ship in an orderly fashion until they saw
us arrive; then it was every man for himself. No one bothered to fire on us. We took out
the radio antenna...One lifeboat capsized as a host of sailors tried to use each other to
climb aboard; two others made it safely in the water...As we left the area to pursue other
game, we saw more people on the beach.
—Reinhard Hardegen, Captain's Log, U-123, April 11, 1942

War came quickly to the Sunshine State following the Japanese attack on Pearl Harbor. Benito Mussolini and Adolph Hitler, bound by the Tripartite Treaty to support the Empire of Japan, declared war on the United States on December 11, 1941. Mussolini's decision to go to war had little immediate impact, but Hitler unleashed an onslaught of violence along America's eastern coastline. Although Germany lacked the ability to bomb or invade the United States, it had a large and effective submarine force that could and did exact a heavy toll on ships. Within days of Hitler's proclamation, Admiral Karl Donitz, the commander of the German U-boat fleet, dispatched five submarines to take up stations off the American coast and to attack any ships they found. Although the United States Navy had been engaged in an undeclared war with German submarines attacking convoys of cargo ships to the United Kingdom and had lost a four-stacker destroyer, the USS *Reuben James* and 115 sailors to a U-boat on October 31, 1941, neither country admitted to engaging in open warfare. The declaration of war changed that. On January 11, 1942, barely a month after Pearl Harbor, Reinhard Hardegen and *U-123* sank the SS *Cyclops*, the first of four hundred ships in American waters sent to the bottom.

Operation Drumbeat (*Paukenschlag*) took Americans by surprise. Cities along the Atlantic coast failed to implement the most basic of wartime measures, and no blackouts were ordered. The brightly lit cities were welcomed navigational aids for U-boat commanders, and the glow of city lights often silhouetted passing ships. The first wave of U-boat attacks was limited to the coast between Cape Hatteras and the St. Lawrence River, and when it ended on February 6, twenty-five ships, totaling more than 156,000 tons, had been sunk. As soon as the first wave ended, more German submarines were on station, and the hunting grounds extended farther south to Key West.

The American response to coastal attacks by U-boats was slow in coming. Admiral Ernest King, who had been appointed commander in chief of the U.S. fleet on December 30, 1941, refused to adopt a convoy system for coastal shipping. Instead, he assigned antisubmarine patrols to the navy and Coast Guard, but these proved largely ineffective because they followed set schedules, which were soon recorded by German submariners, who planned their attacks around them. The U.S. Navy had at its disposal a limited number of warships, most of which were primarily involved in escorting convoys to Great Britain and Russia, and so American coastal defenses were left to a hodgepodge of antiquated airplanes, cutters and gunboats.

Given the success of the initial German effort in the face of such a tepid American response, Admiral Donitz freed his U-boats to hunt up and down the entire Atlantic coast. Slowly, the submarine menace moved toward Florida. The second wave of Operation Drumbeat had started, and over the next four months it would claim more than twenty-five ships off the coast of the state between February and May 1942.

On February 19, 1942, the SS *Pan Massachusetts*, a slow tanker carrying a cargo of Texas oil, became the first victim of Operation Drumbeat in Florida waters. *U-128*, commanded by *Korvettenkapitan* Ulrich Heyse, sent two torpedoes into its hull at 1:45 p.m., just 20 miles east of Cape Canaveral. Twenty of the thirty-eight crew members aboard perished when the lifeboats caught fire and burned. The British tanker *Elizabeth Massey* was nearby and, along with the Coast Guard buoy tender *Forward*, arrived on the scene within minutes and took survivors on board. Two days later, Heyse and the *U-128* struck again when they sank the SS *Cities Service Empire* not far away from the site of the U-boat's first victim. On February 21, *U-504* sank the tanker *Republic*, which went aground about 3 miles from the Jupiter Lighthouse. Forty-eight hours later, the *U-504* scored again when it sent the *W.D. Anderson*, another tanker loaded with 134,000 gallons of crude oil, to the bottom about 12 miles northeast of the lighthouse. Thirty-five of the thirty-six crew members aboard perished. A third ship, the Dutch tanker *Mamura*, fell victim to the *U-504* on February 26, 230 miles off the coast.

Table 1
PARTIAL LIST OF SHIPS SUNK IN FLORIDA WATERS
February–May 1942

NAME	DATE SUNK	CASUALTIES
Pan Massachusetts	February 19	20
Republic	February 21	5
Cities Service Empire	February 22	14
W.D. Anderson	February 22	35
Mamura	February 26	49
GulfAmerica	April 11	19
Leslie	April 12	4
Korsholm	April 13	9
La Paz	May 1	0
Ocean Venus	May 3	5
Laertes	May 3	18
Eclipse	May 4	2

NAME	DATE SUNK	CASUALTIES
Norlindo	May 4	5
Delisle	May 5	0
Amazone	May 6	14
Halsey	May 6	0
Java Arrow	May 6	2
Ohioan	May 8	15

Undeterred by the feeble efforts of the Coast Guard and navy to stop them, the U-boats continued to range freely along the American coast into the Gulf of Mexico and throughout the Caribbean. Urban myths about small groups of German submariners coming ashore to purchase fresh milk, bread or vegetables quickly sprang up. One myth declared that Germans had come ashore at Jupiter, purchased supplies from several small stores and finished their adventure by taking in a movie at the local theatre. Did such things happen? Historian Michael Gannon, author of *Operation Drumbeat: The Dramatic True Story of Germany's First U-boat Attacks along the American Coast in World War II*, denies any such escapades and points to the lack of any mention of them in the official logs of the U-boats. There are, however, scores of people who stoutly maintain that Germans did come ashore and cite as their proof personal experiences. The question is still a very controversial one.

On Highway A1A, near the Palmetto Park Pavilion in Boca Raton, a historical marker at the site of Dr. William Sanborn's house (now demolished) marks the discovery of "a telescope, signaling device, and other evidence that spies had occupied the vacant home." In 2006, author Sally J. Ling popularized this tale in a children's book, *Phillip's Great Adventure—Spies, Root Beer and Alligators*. The fifteen hundred miles of Florida's beaches offered an open invitation to spies and saboteurs. Coast Guard and navy personnel conducted daily patrols of Florida's beaches, often on horseback. But even the most diligent efforts of military and civilian patrollers could not prevent a determined foe, as evidenced by the June 1942 landing of four saboteurs on Ponte Vedra Beach.

By the end of May 1942, however, Admiral King had begun to organize his military resources and thousands of civilian volunteers to create a coordinated submarine watch from Maine to Key West. In addition, the

Navy beach patrols, often mounted on horseback, regularly patrolled Florida's beaches to prevent Nazi U-boats from landing spies or conducting spying operations. This patrol was from the Mayport Naval Station near Jacksonville. *Courtesy of the Beaches Historical Society, Jacksonville Beach.*

Established in 1939, the Banana River Naval Air Station (NAS) in Brevard County was home to amphibious aircraft that conducted antisubmarine patrols along the Atlantic shore. Later, the Banana River NAS was also used to train pilots to fly the large amphibious planes that kept the shipping lanes clear of U-boats. *Courtesy of the Florida Historical Society.*

Large wooden towers were constructed on the beaches of the Sunshine State as part of the military's antisubmarine watch. Often manned by civilian volunteers, these towers provided views of stretches of the ocean several miles wide. Similar towers were built inland to provided aircraft spotters a clear view of the sky. *Courtesy of the Florida Photographic Collection.*

navy began flying submarine patrols from the coastal bases it had established. In Florida, flights from NAS Jacksonville, NAS Banana River, NAS Vero Beach, NAS Palm Beach and other installations added hundreds of aircraft to the job of patrolling. Student pilots often flew training missions over the ocean, learning necessary skills but also keeping a close eye out for U-boats.

Watchtowers were built on isolated beaches, and civilian volunteers manned these lonely outposts around the clock. Civilian pilots flew daily patrols in their private airplanes, while boat owners crewed a variety of craft—from yachts to small fishing boats—on antisubmarine patrols. Novelist Ernest Hemingway contributed to the war against U-boats by conducting regular patrols in the waters between Cuba and Key West in his fishing boat, *Pilar*. The Federal Bureau of Investigation, particularly Director J. Edgar Hoover, was sure that Hemingway's patrols were much more than fishing trips using government gas. Publicity about his patrols stimulated others to volunteer their time and boats for patrolling.

Volunteer aircraft spotters manned the steeples of churches and cupolas of courthouses to keep watch for enemy planes. Tall wooden towers, just like those built for beach watchers, were constructed in open pastures and wooded areas, ideal locations to watch the skies. Volunteers, equipped with telephones, reported suspicious activity with an "Army Flash," which connected them to a central clearinghouse for such reports.

The probable presence of spies or fifth columnists worried most Americans. On the same day Japan attacked Pearl Harbor, President Roosevelt issued Presidential Proclamation 2525, which designated resident German and Japanese citizens as "aliens" subject to roundup and incarceration. This presidential proclamation was followed up by two additional proclamations on December 8, which further defined their status. All citizens of Germany, Italy and Japan or resident aliens from these countries were required to report to federal authorities and to register with them. No alien could possess shortwave radios or other signaling devices, weapons, ammunition or cameras, nor could they travel in areas that were designated as restricted.

In Florida, military authorities in the Seventh Naval District, headquartered in Jacksonville, and the Eighth Naval District in Pensacola were given responsibility for regulating the activities of Italian fishermen, whose boats were either confiscated or operated under the close watch of authorities. Although Florida did not have a large population of foreigners, there were pockets of Germans, Italians and Japanese scattered around the

A gun crew from the Mayport Naval Station sights its antiaircraft gun on the beach. Responsible for the security of a large area of coastal beaches, naval personnel at the base were constantly training and patrolling. *Courtesy of the Beaches Historical Society, Jacksonville Beach.*

Jacksonville Beach was a popular recreation destination for civilians and service personnel in the Jacksonville area. A large crowd such as this was at the beach and witnessed the U-boat attack on the tanker SS *GulfAmerica* on April 10, 1942. *Courtesy of the Beaches Historical Society, Jacksonville Beach.*

The *La Paz*, a freighter carrying whiskey and china, was torpedoed off Cocoa Beach by a German U-boat. Local high school students were asked to help salvage its cargo of nine hundred cases of Johnny Walker scotch. A considerable number of the bottles was buried under the sand and retrieved later at night by the students. The *La Paz* was refloated and went back into service. It was torpedoed twice more during the war but refloated each time. *Courtesy of the Florida Historical Society.*

Although most freighters were eventually armed with deck guns to use against U-boats, they were largely ineffective. This is the forward gun mount on the *La Paz. Courtesy of the Florida Historical Society*.

state. In Tampa, the cigar industry in Ybor City attracted a considerable number of Italians, while the Yamato Colony near Boca Raton was home to a small number of Japanese. Nevertheless, federal authorities proceeded with registering aliens, conducting raids on their homes and arresting small numbers who were suspected of being spies.

On February 19, 1942, Roosevelt broadened the scope of his earlier presidential proclamation and issued Executive Order 9066. This order authorized the creation of exclusion zones (roughly one-third of the land area of the United States), in which persons of certain national origins could not reside. Under this order, a few resident aliens were detained at a detention facility in Miami, but the Sunshine State never had any large internment camps like those in the western part of the United States. Nationwide, some 120,000 Japanese Americans, 11,000 persons of German ancestry and 3,000 people of Italian ancestry were rounded up and placed in camps for the duration of the war. Ironically, a few Jewish refugees from Germany were also interned because the federal government did not differentiate between ethnic Jews and ethnic Germans. Few, if any, spies were arrested from among the thousands of detainees.

War Comes to Florida

The Federal Bureau of Investigation, headed by J. Edgar Hoover, was charged with monitoring and curbing spy activities in the United States. In December 1941, just a few days after the Pearl Harbor attack, the FBI arrested thirty-three members of a German spy ring, headed by Frederick Joubert Duquesne, in New York. Throughout the war, the FBI maintained field offices in South America and Europe to keep track of German intelligence agents. To a large degree, the organization was successful in its efforts. Between 1941 and 1945, scores of German spies were arrested, tried before military tribunals and sentenced. Scores of others were arrested, detained for short periods and eventually allowed to go free, but with an admonition that they would remain under close watch. In Florida, even winter visitors in ritzy Palm Beach were not exempt. Two members of the German nobility—Baron Fritz von Opel

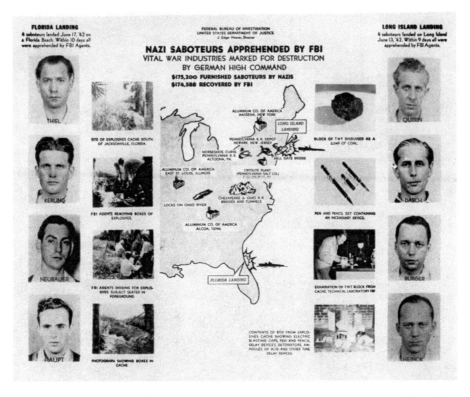

Four German saboteurs landed on the beach near Ponte Vedra on June 17, 1942. Part of Operation Pastorius, they were supposed to join up with four other saboteurs who had landed on Long Island to carry out the sabotage of American industries across the United States. They were caught when one of the men revealed the plan to the Federal Bureau of Investigation. *Courtesy of the Beaches Historical Society, Jacksonville Beach.*

and Countess Erica von Haacke—were arrested, along with members of their families, as "potential dangerous aliens."

The Sunshine State was the setting for one of the most unusual spy dramas of the war. On June 17, 1942, *U-584* slowly surfaced off the coast of Ponte Vedra Beach. Four men boarded a rubber raft and made their way to shore. There, they unloaded four boxes containing explosives and $170,000 in American currency. Hastily digging a hole, they buried their cache after retrieving civilian clothes and a small amount of money. Carefully looking around for any sign that someone had seen them and seeing none, they made their way to an isolated grocery store some three miles from the landing site and purchased bus tickets to Jacksonville. Once there, they registered in two hotels, secure in the knowledge that their "invasion" of the Sunshine State had gone unnoticed. After eating breakfast, the four men bought train tickets for New York and Chicago and, traveling in pairs, set off on their mission.

The saboteurs who landed at Ponte Vedra buried large quantities of explosives and money in a heavily wooded area of the beach. The demolition supplies were later recovered by the FBI. *Courtesy of the Beaches Historical Society, Jacksonville Beach.*

FBI agents examined the neatly wrapped packages of explosives brought ashore by the Ponte Vedra saboteurs. Photographs were made for use in the trial of the saboteurs, which took place before a military tribunal in Washington, D.C. *Courtesy of the Beaches Historical Society, Jacksonville Beach.*

The four men—Edward John Kerling, Herbert Hans Haupt, Werner Thiel and Herman Niebauer—were the second wave of Operation Pastorius, a daring plan to sabotage American industries and to sow terror throughout American cities devised by the Abwehr, the German military intelligence agency. The first wave, also made up of four men, had been put ashore by *U-202* at Amagansett, New York, earlier on June 12. The first team was led by Georg Johann Dasch and included Richard Quirin, Heinrich Heinck and Ernst Burger. The men were recruited because they all spoke English and had previously lived in the United States. Two of them, Burger and Haupt, were American citizens.

After only thirty hours in the United States, Dasch, who was the overall mission commander, decided to surrender to the FBI and reveal the extent of the plot. Although the New York office of the agency refused to believe his story when he called them on the telephone, Dasch traveled to the FBI's home office in Washington and demanded an interview with J. Edgar

Disguised as pieces of coal, these explosives were to be thrown into coal heaps used by trains or industry. They were designed to explode when exposed to heat, and their purpose was to give the saboteurs time to exit an area. *Courtesy of the Beaches Historical Society, Jacksonville Beach.*

The eight German saboteurs of Operation Pastorius were brought before a military tribunal in Washington. All eight were convicted. Six were sentenced to death and executed in the electric chair. Two of the men who had assisted the FBI were given life sentences, which were later commuted. They were repatriated to the American zone in Occupied Germany after the war. *Courtesy of the Beaches Historical Society, Jacksonville Beach.*

Hoover. When Hoover refused to meet with him, Dasch surrendered a packet containing $80,000 to skeptical agents, who immediately took a new interest in his story. Although the second group of saboteurs had not yet landed in Florida, the FBI was alerted. Within two weeks, all eight saboteurs were arrested and their caches confiscated. Dasch and Ernst Burger cooperated with the agency to help catch the other men.

Tried before a secret military commission in Washington, the men were all convicted of espionage, sabotage and conspiracy and found guilty. Six of the men were put to death in the electric chair in the District of Columbia, while Dasch and Burger received prison terms. They were repatriated to the American zone in Occupied Germany after the war. Although the press was prevented from attending the trial of the eight men, newspapers were filled with accounts of the landings and captures.

War had indeed come to the Sunshine State.

Chapter 5

"The Biggest Damned Aircraft Carrier in the World"

For conspicuous leadership above the call of duty, involving personal valor and intrepidity at an extreme hazard to life. With the apparent certainty of being forced to land in enemy territory or to perish at sea, General Doolittle personally led a squadron of Army bombers, manned by volunteer crews, in a highly destructive raid on the Japanese mainland.
Medal of Honor Citation, General James H. Doolittle, 1942

It was understood that there had to be some sort of response, if for nothing else than to lift American morale. But more importantly it was necessary to show Japan that they were not untouchable. Exposing their vulnerability was in itself a major part of the operation. I was under no illusion that we would strike any major blow with regard to tactical, let alone strategic damage with our bombers. The purpose was psychological all the way around, and I think it worked. I know it worked for our nation.
—Interview with General James H. Doolittle

Smarting at the success of the Japanese sneak attack on Pearl Harbor, President Franklin Roosevelt asked the heads of the armed services to devise a quick and effective strike against Japan that would raise the morale of the American population. General Henry H. "Hap" Arnold, chief of the United States Air Corps (later the U.S. Army Air Forces), approved a plan developed by Major James H. Doolittle, a reserve officer in the group assigned to develop a response. What he proposed was Special Mission No. 1, an air attack on the Japanese homeland by Mitchell bombers (B-25s), which would take off from the deck of the carrier *Hornet* cruising some four hundred to five hundred miles off Japan's shores. The plan was an audacious one, since no one had ever flown a bomber from a carrier, but two test flights proved that it could be done. Several cities—Tokyo, Yokohama, Yokosuka, Nagoya, Kobe and Osaka—were targeted with the objective of demonstrating that the Japanese homeland was not impervious to attack and to cause a great "loss of face" for the empire's military. The plan called for American bombers to overfly Japan, drop their bombs and proceed to friendly territory on the mainland of China. Physical damage would be minimal, but the psychological impact on the Japanese psyche was expected to be devastating. Arnold approved the plan and asked Doolittle to command it.

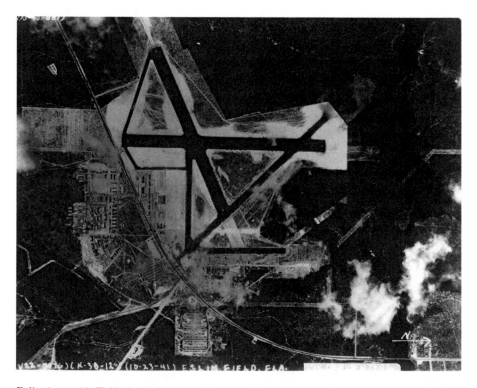

Eglin Army Air Field, shown here in 1941, would become one of the most active airfields in the Sunshine State, quite a dramatic change from its beginning as a small municipal airport. *Courtesy of Eglin Air Force Museum.*

"The Biggest Damned Aircraft Carrier in the World"

With planes and crews drawn from the Seventeenth Bombardment Group, Doolittle arrived at Eglin Field near Valparaiso, Florida, in early March 1942. Under the watchful eye of Lieutenant Henry Miller, the crews practiced takeoffs on an isolated runway at nearby Hurlburt Field marked with white lines to approximate the length of a carrier deck. In addition, crews were given intensive training on cross-country and over-water navigation, bombing at various altitudes and night flying to give them experience for the mission. Gunners and maintenance crews also received training at Eglin. On March 25, with training completed, the planes took off for California, where the final modifications to the aircraft were made.

Sixteen B-25s were loaded onto the deck of the USS *Hornet* on April 1, 1942, and the carrier and its escort force departed Alameda Naval Air Station the next day. For more than two weeks, the task force steamed toward Japan. On April 17, after the task force was sighted by a Japanese picket boat, the decision was made to launch early. The planes encountered little antiaircraft fire and only minimal resistance by Japanese fighters as they bombed their targets and proceeded toward China. Fifteen of the sixteen crash-landed or their crews bailed out, and the sixteenth landed in Russia. Of the eighty men on the mission, eight were captured by Japanese forces. Four of the captured aviators were executed, but the remaining four survived the war. The remaining crews eventually made their way back to friendly forces.

The leader, James H. Doolittle, was one of the survivors. He was promoted from lieutenant colonel to brigadier general, awarded the Medal of Honor and assigned to the Eighth Air Force. He subsequently commanded the Twelfth Air Force in North Africa, the Fifteenth Air Force and the Eighth Air Force. After the war, he was a vice-president with Shell Oil, although he continued to serve in a number of advisory roles for the military and the federal government.

The Sunshine State had proven to be a popular pilot training venue in World War I. So the choice of Eglin Field as the training site for Doolittle's Raiders was a logical one. The base, located in the sparsely populated Florida Panhandle, came to life in 1933 as the Valparaiso (Municipal) Airport, a small, 137-acre site with no paved runways or outbuildings. In March 1935, city officials applied for a FERA (Federal Emergency Relief Administration) grant to pave the runways and to add barracks and a mess hall. In June 1935, the small airport and a surrounding 1,460 acres of land became the Valparaiso Bombing and Gunnery Base. On August 4, 1937, the installation

Eglin Army Air Field in 1942. In less than a year, a significant number of new hangars, barracks and administrative buildings had changed the airfield from a small base into a major military installation. *Courtesy of Eglin Air Force Museum.*

was renamed Eglin Field in honor of Lieutenant Colonel Frederick Irving Eglin, an aviator who was killed in an airplane crash. In 1939, a decision was made to expand Eglin as a proving ground for aircraft armaments, and the War Department acquired the entire Choctawhatchee National Forest, some 340,890 acres in southern Okaloosa, Walton and Santa Rosa Counties. In addition, the United States Army Air Forces claimed four thousand square miles of the Gulf of Mexico. The isolation of the base and its sheer size also guaranteed complete secrecy for the Doolittle mission training. The same qualities make it one of the U.S. Air Force's premier bases today.

On May 15, 1941, the Air Corps Proving Ground (later the Proving Ground Command) was activated, and Eglin became the site for gunnery training for Army Air Forces fighter pilots, as well as a major testing center for aircraft, equipment and tactics. The Twenty-third Composite Group—comprising the First Pursuit Squadron, the Fifty-fourth Bombardment Squadron, the Twenty-fourth Bombardment Squadron, the Fifty-fourth School Squadron, the Sixty-first Air Base Group and the Third Gunnery and Bombing Range Detachment—moved from Orlando Army Airfield to Eglin Field on July 1, 1941.

Eglin Field was just one of the more than twenty Army Air Forces installations that dotted the Florida countryside during World War II. In addition, there were numerous smaller, non-flying commands scattered around the state, including the officer candidate training center on Miami Beach. Virtually every airplane in the American arsenal was flown in the Sunshine State, and more than one million pilot trainees, including thousands from Allied countries, received their first exposure to aircraft here. The vast expanses of Florida flatlands, the large sections of sparsely inhabited countryside and the endless number of clear days and nights provided an excellent classroom for training. Some of the bases—like Eglin—were huge, while others occupied only a few hundred acres. Auxiliary fields and bombing ranges took up additional acreage. By the end of 1942, there were so many planes in the air over Florida that one wag pronounced it to be "a floating fortress—the biggest damned aircraft carrier in the world."

Floridians welcomed the arrival of the USAAF because the thousands of airmen (and women) stationed at each of these bases pumped millions of dollars into the local economy. Likewise, civilians found ready employment on the bases, undertaking a variety of tasks that otherwise would have demanded military personnel. Following so closely on the heels of the New Deal, the outbreak of war and the influx of service personnel, to say nothing of the availability of good jobs, ended the Depression in the Sunshine State several years before other southern states could claim that.

Tampa benefited more than any other Florida city from the entry of the United States into World War II. TASCO, Hooker's Point, Tampa Marine Company and Bushnell-Lyons, another small company, produced a variety of ships and provided employment for some thirty-one thousand workers by war's end. In addition to these facilities, Tampa was also home to three major airfields—MacDill Field, Drew Field and Hillsborough Army Airfield—which trained thousands of pilots and crews for B-24, B-25, B-26 and B-17 bombers. Across Tampa Bay in Clearwater, the Pinellas Army Airfield (now the Clearwater International Airport) served as an adjunct field to the larger MacDill Field.

Dedicated on April 16, 1941, and named in honor of Colonel Leslie MacDill, an army aviator who was killed in an airplane crash in 1938, MacDill Field was initially the home of two bomber groups that flew

Drew Army Air Field, now Tampa International Airport, was one of three major pilot training bases in the immediate Tampa area. From late 1943 until 1945, Drew AAF was home to a large contingent of German POWs. *Courtesy of the Anthony Pizzo Collection, University of South Florida Special Collections.*

The B-24 Liberator, an American heavy bomber, was a familiar sight in the skies around Tampa Bay as thousands of fledgling pilots took to the air. *Courtesy of the Sebring Historical Society.*

P.1231 Boeing "B-17-E" Largest and Most Deadly of the Flying Fortresses

The B-17 Flying Fortress was the premier American bomber against Axis targets in Europe. The British flew night raids against German cities, while the Americans, with their heavily armed B-17s, flew raids during daylight hours. The Sebring AAF was a major training base for B-17 pilots. *Courtesy of the Sebring Historical Society.*

Nose art, ranging from the moderate to the risqué, frequently decorated American bombers. Lieutenant Irving Rubin flew this B-24, *My Bill*, over Europe. He flew it back to the United States when the war was over. *Courtesy of the Irving Rubin Collection, the Florida Historical Society.*

Pilots also trained to fly the medium Curtiss B-26 Marauder bomber at bases in the Tampa area. Student pilots called the B-26 the "Widow Maker" because of the large number of accidents inexperienced air cadets had during attempted takeoffs. It was used in all theatres of the war by Allied units and was a favorite of pilots—once they learned how to get it off the ground safely. *Courtesy of the Avon Park Air Force Range.*

antisubmarine missions over the Gulf of Mexico, the Caribbean and the Atlantic from January 1941 until June 1942. Additional groups stationed at the base included two commands that ferried bombers to the Pacific and the Fifty-third Pursuit Group, which provided fighter protection for American planes. When the United States entered World War II, MacDill became a training base, teaching fledgling pilots the intricacies of flying heavy bombers of all types. The skies over the Cigar City were filled with planes twenty-four hours a day, and residents became inured to the heavy pounding of plane engines. Accidents by student pilots were so common that pilots and civilians alike cavalierly dismissed them with the oft-quoted refrain, "One a day in Tampa Bay."

The presence of such a large population of transients in Tampa had a distinctive influence on local society. Civic-minded men and women volunteered thousands of hours of their time to provide entertainment and critical services. In nearby St. Petersburg, the "Bomb-a-Dears," a group of 445 local women between the ages of eighteen and thirty, served as hostesses and dance partners at events throughout the Tampa Bay area. Of course, there was a darker side to the presence of so many unattached men, and local authorities had great difficulty controlling the growth of bars, gambling and prostitution. "Victory girls," who came to the city to work in industry and adopted the "live-for-today" philosophy that the uncertainty of war produced, exacerbated the problems. Although they were not prostitutes necessarily, they often freely engaged in sexual escapades with servicemen and added to the growing venereal disease problem. Tampa was not the only Florida city to face a raging venereal disease problem. Throughout the Sunshine State, public health officials and military physicians tried to come to grips with the rising rates of gonorrhea and syphilis that originated outside military bases and spread through the cities and into the countryside. What was true in Tampa was true elsewhere.

There were other large USAAF bases in the Sunshine State engaged in the training of airmen. In December 1940, a site board determined that

Local young women attended dances at the USO clubs around military bases. This photograph was taken at the Tampa USO sometime in 1943. *Courtesy of the Hampton Dunn Collection, University of South Florida Special Collections.*

Soldiers on passes from local bases flocked to nearby towns to see what they could see. Often they met young ladies and struck up friendships. This is the corner of Polk and Cass Streets in Tampa, the home of Happy's Corner, one of the favorite hangouts for soldiers. *Courtesy of the Hampton Dunn Collection, University of South Florida Special Collections.*

Flexible Gunnery School No. 9 would be located twelve miles southeast of Panama City, Florida, on the East Peninsula. On May 6, 1941, army and local dignitaries held an official groundbreaking for the school. Panama City's mayor, Harry Fannin, dug the first spade of sand, and Colonel Warren Maxwell, Tyndall's first commander, wielded the first axe on the stubborn palmetto plants so common on the East Peninsula. The site was covered with pine and palmetto trees, scrub brush and swamps, and bulldozers worked around the clock to clear the brush and fill in swamps. Originally a small base of a few hundred acres, the base would eventually grow to more than twenty-eight thousand acres. On June 13, 1941, the War Department officially named the new installation Tyndall Field in honor of Lieutenant Francis B. Tyndall, a native of Sewall Point, who was a fighter pilot during World War I and was credited with shooting down four German planes in 1918.

STUDENT GUNNERS FIRING AT MINIATURE AIRPLANE AT TYNDALL FIELD NEAR PANAMA CITY, FLORIDA   122-P

Tyndall Army Air Field, located near Panama City, was home to USAAF gunnery students, in addition to students from the Chinese Nationalist Air Force and the Free French Air Force. *Courtesy of the Bay County Library.*

On December 7, 1941, the first of two thousand troops arrived at Tyndall Field. Although construction was incomplete, instructors and students began preparing for the first class. The first class of forty gunnery students began on February 23, 1942. Of the thousands of students passing through the Tyndall gates, Clark Gable, a student here during 1943, was the most famous. That same year, the USAAF accepted its first class of foreign students when the Free French Air Force sent a small group of men for gunnery training. A class of Chinese students from Generalissimo Chiang Kai Shek's Kuomintang Nationalist Air Force, which was heavily engaged in fighting the Japanese and the Chinese Communists, also underwent training at Tyndall.

In Orlando, the USAAF built two bases. Orlando Army Airfield, located on what is now the Orlando Executive Airport, became the major training center for the Army Air Force School of Applied Tactics in late 1940. By mid-1943, the base was also home to a pilot training school for the gigantic B-29 Superfortress bomber. The Orlando AAF command also operated five additional sub bases—Ocala Army Airfield, Leesburg Army Airfield, Alachua Army Airfield, Keystone Heights Army Airfield and Orlando

Popular movie star Clark Gable, an officer in the Army Air Force, was among the trainees who learned gunnery at Tyndall Army Air Field. Locals still remember his visits to Panama City. *Courtesy of the Bay County Library.*

"The Biggest Damned Aircraft Carrier in the World"

O-6—Entrance to Orlando Air Base, Orlando, Fla.

Orlando Air Force Base was a large base with secondary bases located in several smaller towns. It was the principal training base for applied tactics and chemical weapons testing. *Courtesy of the Orange County Regional History Center.*

Army Airfield Number Two, which eventually became the Pinecastle Army Airfield, located on the site of the present-day Orlando International Airport. Pinecastle AAF became the major testing site for chemical weapons and other new technologies for the USAAF. The AAFSAT command also claimed control of an eight-thousand-square-mile training course that stretched from Apalachicola in the panhandle to Titusville on the Atlantic coast and to Ocala and Gainesville.

Some Florida counties had multiple bases. In rural Lee County (Fort Myers), Buckingham Army Airfield was dedicated in 1942 and initially had only 650 acres, but by 1945, it encompassed some 75,000 acres, including its bombing ranges. Complete with moving targets, a faux town that served to give student pilots experience on urban targets and various other kinds of "real life" targets, the base processed some forty-eight thousand students during its three-year existence.

Hendricks Army Airfield in Sebring became one of the most active bases in the Sunshine State. The Army Air Forces created the base in a hurry in 1940. Within a year, however, the base was operational, and a steady stream of B-17s roared down its runways and into the Florida skies. Nearby Avon Park Army Airfield, with its large bombing range and gunnery targets,

When the first of what would become hundreds of Army Air Force bombers landed at the Orlando AAF, it was big news. This early photograph shows the first plane to land at the base. *Courtesy of the Orange County Regional History Center.*

This is the headquarters building for the United States Army Air Forces Tactical Center at Orlando AAF. From this center, combat tactics were put into operation and tested for their value to frontline pilots, chemical weapons and other specialized weapons were tested at outlying sub bases and innovative new combat techniques were created. *Courtesy of the Jack Rabun Postcard Collection.*

The quarters for married enlisted personnel at Hendricks Field in Sebring. Neat and orderly, these small homes allowed personnel stationed at the base to maintain a normal home life during the war. *Courtesy of the Sebring Historical Society.*

provided excellent opportunities for pilots and bombardiers to refine critical skills they would need in battle. Lake Arbuckle on the Avon Park base featured a large wooden mock-up of a German U-boat to provide pilots and their crews with experience bombing submarines at sea. A large contingent of WAAFs and WACs was assigned to the base throughout the war. Garrison troops assisted contractors building necessary barracks and hangars and even painted murals inside the base chapels. The military employed a large number of specially trained photographers to record activities on the base and to supply propaganda pictures for media outlets. Hendricks Field was closed as an active military base in 1946, but it is used today as Sebring's municipal airport.

Fort Myers Army Airfield evolved out of a municipal airport, Page Field, owned by the City of Fort Myers. The 670 acres of land were originally purchased for a municipal golf course in 1923, but that plan was halted when the Florida "bust" stopped development. From 1927 until 1937, Page Field was used by National Airlines as a stopover for planes on its St. Petersburg–

The afternoon ceremony of lowering the flag on the main flagpole at Hendricks AAF in Sebring. This publicity was deliberately posed to show how civilians and the military worked together as a unit to keep the base operational. *Courtesy of the Sebring Historical Society.*

Miami run. In 1937, the Works Project Administration constructed three long, concrete runways. On March 31, 1942, the USAAF took control of the airport and renamed it the Fort Myers Army Airfield. Initially, the base was used as home to two bomber-training groups that used the nearby Buckingham Field bombing ranges, but by early 1943, the airbase was being used to train fighter pilots to fly P-39, P-47, P-40 and P-51 fighters. It closed in early 1946, and the airfield again reverted to being a civilian airport.

Sarasota County was also home to two USAAF bases. Leased to the Army Air Corps in early 1942, the newly constructed Sarasota Bradenton Airport became Sarasota Army Airfield. Originally a sub base of MacDill AAF in Tampa and used for heavy bomber training, the runways proved to be unable to bear the weight of such heavy planes, so the mission of the base changed to training pilots for the P-39 Airacobra fighter.

Venice, a small Florida boomtown in southern Sarasota County, was home to the Venice Army Airfield, which opened in December 1942. Primarily a

Enlisted personnel at Hendricks AAF painted murals in all of the base chapels. Note the figures of troops engaged in combat around the edges of the mural. A pilot, with his goggles atop his leather helmet, is in the upper left corner. *Courtesy of the Sebring Historical Society.*

training facility for airplane mechanics, the base had more than four thousand military and civilian personnel filling the various engine schools from Rollison, Republic, Rolls-Royce and Pratt. In addition, some four hundred men from the Fourteenth Chinese Service Group were trained to fly the P-40 Warhawk. Airmen were also used as rescue crews for downed pilots in the Gulf of Mexico and for salvage work recovering equipment from sunken planes. American pilots flew P-47 and P-51 fighters on antisubmarine patrols over the Gulf. Beginning in 1943, some two hundred German and Italian prisoners of war from Camp Blanding were used in a variety of maintenance jobs on the base, including mess duty in the officers' dining room.

Nearby Punta Gorda was also home to a small air force base. The Punta Gorda Airfield was constructed in 1943 and used as a training facility for Army Air Corps pilots receiving instruction in flying P-40 and, later, P-51 fighter aircraft. The Twenty-seventh Service Group, an all-black unit, was relocated from MacDill Field in Tampa to provide training for support services to air combat units.

Pilots and base personnel attend this theatrically staged Easter sunrise service at Hendricks AAF in Sebring in 1943 or 1944. *Courtesy of the Sebring Historical Society.*

One of the most active USAAF installations in Florida was Morrison Field, which opened in 1936 as the Air Transport Command. With the outbreak of war, Morrison Field became the point of departure for many planes that were ferrying supplies to Europe and to Allied forces in the Asian theatre. Home to about 3,000 service personnel during the war, Morrison Field counted some 250 members of the Women's Army Corps (WAC) among its permanent staff. It is estimated that some 45,000 pilots either trained at Morrison Field or flew out of the base. Morrison Field also served as a major supply and repair facility during the war. More than 1,000 men worked around the clock to repair, replace and test engines to keep the transports flying. Throughout the war, a veil of secrecy cloaked the activities on Morrison Field because authorities wanted to prevent spies from knowing the arrival and departure times of cargo planes, as well as their destinations.

Nearby, the USAAF opened the Boca Raton Army Airfield on October 12, 1942, as a school to teach operators for the new airborne radar systems in use by the military. In addition to teaching operators, the base was responsible for installing these systems on American aircraft and for training pilots for the heavy B-17 bombers that were wreaking havoc on Germany. In addition to learning to fly, cadets spent long hours each day in classroom situations learning navigation, math, military courtesy and other necessary skills.

Utilizing four long runways to service arriving planes and to provide for training flights, the base operated twenty-four hours a day. More than 10,000 service personnel were assigned to the airfield, and an estimated 100,000 troops were trained there or passed through the base en route to other destinations. The USAAF constructed more than eight hundred buildings to handle the sheer volume of people and personnel. African American troops provided much of the necessary support staff for operations at the Boca Raton Airfield, and the USAAF created a school on the post to teach them about aircraft engine repair and maintenance. Black soldiers were segregated as Squadron F, and their housing, meals, training and recreation were all separate from the white soldiers.

During the early stages of World War II, the United States needed air bases along the Florida coasts to keep tabs on German submarine operations and to provide stopover bases for aircraft being ferried to North Africa and the Caribbean. On September 16, 1942, the USAAF took control of a small airport near Biscayne Bay and named it Homestead Army Airfield. For the first six months of its existence, the base was used as a stopover for planes on their way elsewhere and as an antisubmarine patrol base. In January 1943, the base also became a training facility for student pilots learning to fly transport planes. By the middle of 1943, training pilots had become the sole mission of the base. By mid-1945, the base had graduated 16,755 pilots and copilots for the four-engine C-54 transport, plus an additional 1,684 navigators, flight engineers and radio operators.

Homestead AAF's wartime use came to a screeching halt on September 15, 1945—three years to the day after its opening—when a massive hurricane packing 145-miles-an-hour winds demolished a major portion of the buildings on the base. However, by then, Japan had surrendered and the war was over. The base officially closed on December 14, 1945.

There were other, smaller USAAF bases in the Sunshine State. Scattered around the state were a number of small auxiliary and special use fields—Carlstrom AAF in Arcadia, Brooksville AAF in Brooksville, Hendricks AAF in Sebring, Lakeland AAF in Lakeland and Marianna AAF in Marianna—that were sub bases of the larger installations.

In addition, a number of emergency landing fields and fighter bases—Conners Field in Okeechobee, Imokalee Municipal Airport in Imokalee—were maintained by the USAAF. Avon Park Bombing Range, later Avon Park Army Airfield; Pinecastle Jeep Range, later Pinecastle AAF; Mullet Key in Pinellas County; and several ranges on larger air bases provided targets for student pilots.

The large number of USAAF bases and the thousands of pilots who learned to fly in the Sunshine State were matched by an equal number of navy bases, which provided pilot training to additional thousands. During World War II, Florida truly was "a floating fortress—the biggest damned aircraft carrier in the world."

Table 2

UNITED STATES ARMY AIR FORCE BASES IN FLORIDA
1930–1945

CITY	BASE	YEAR FOUNDED	SIZE (ACRES)
Avon Park	Avon Park Bombing Range	1942	220,000
	Avon Park Army Airfield	1943	Same
Bartow	Bartow Army Airfield	1942	900
Boca Raton	Boca Raton Army Airfield	1942	5,820
Brooksville	Brooksville Army Airfield	1942	2,014
Clearwater	Pinellas Army Airfield	1942	Unknown
Dade County	Homestead Army Airfield	1942	Unknown
Fort Myers	Buckingham Army Airfield	1942	75,000
	Page Army Airfield	1942	670
Gainesville	Alachua Army Airfield	1942	1,650
Keystone Heights	Keystone Heights Army Airfield	1942	2,505
Lakeland	Lakeland Army Airfield (later Drane Field)	1942	Unknown
Marianna	Marianna Army Air Base	1942	2,500
Miami	Homestead Army Airfield	1942	Unknown

"The Biggest Damned Aircraft Carrier in the World"

CITY	BASE	YEAR FOUNDED	SIZE (ACRES)
Ocala	Ocala Army Airfield	1942	1,532
Orlando	Orlando Army Airfield	1940	Unknown
	Pinecastle Army Airfield	1940	2,116
Panama City	Tyndall Army Airfield	1941	28,000
Punta Gorda	Punta Gorda Army Airfield	1943	Unknown
Sarasota	Sarasota Army Airfield	1942	870
Sebring	Hendricks Army Airfield*	1941	9,200
Tampa	MacDill Army Air Base	1939	12,200
	Hillsborough Army Airfield	1942	Unknown
	Drew Field	1942	Unknown
Valparaiso	Eglin Army Airfield**	1935	345,000
Venice	Venice Army Airfield	1943	1,600
West Palm Beach	Morrison Army Airfield	1942	1,600

*Auxiliary fields were located at Conners Field in Okeechobee and Imokalee Municipal Airport.

**Ten additional auxiliary fields, plus four thousand square miles of the Gulf of Mexico.

Note: This table does not include additional auxiliary fields or bombing ranges.

Chapter 6

FLORIDA TAKES TO
THE OCEANS

Naval Bases

*Generation after generation, America has battled for the general policy of the freedom of
the seas. And that policy is a very simple one, but a basic, a fundamental one. It means
that no nation has the right to make the broad oceans of the world at great distances from
the actual theatre of land war, unsafe for the commerce of others. That has been our
policy, proved time and [time] again, in all of our history. Our policy has applied from
[time immemorial] the earliest days of the Republic—and still applies—not merely
to the Atlantic but to the Pacific and to all other oceans as well.
—Franklin Delano Roosevelt, September 11, 1941*

President Franklin D. Roosevelt, keenly aware of the dramatic rearmament
of Germany in the mid-1930s and the increasing aggressiveness of the
Japanese military, quietly began to expand the armed forces of the United
States. Naval planners, looking ahead at the possible evolution of naval
warfare and drawing on the doctrines of General Billy Mitchell, urged the
construction of more aircraft carriers and the expansion of programs to
train naval aviators. In 1935, the War Department located the naval air
cadet program to Naval Air Station Pensacola and set about training pilots
for service aboard the slowly growing fleet of aircraft carriers.

Naval Air Station (NAS) Pensacola, which had been the center for naval
aviation since World War I, accepted the first class of aviation cadets on

July 20, 1935. The number of cadets brought into the training program exceeded the ability of NAS Pensacola, so similar training programs were established at NAS Jacksonville and NAS Corpus Christi. However, NAS Pensacola remained the primary training facility and earned the nickname "Annapolis of the Air." Over the next five years, the program expanded, and when war came on December 7, 1941, the navy counted fifty-nine hundred pilots available to fly its 5,233 airplanes. The need was clear: more pilots were needed to fly the new planes, and they would surely come from American factories. Between 1939 and 1945, the U.S. Navy constructed a number of air stations (NAS) and smaller auxiliary air stations (NAAS) in Florida to train pilots in every aspect of naval aviation—from carrier fighting to antisubmarine warfare (ASW) in specially equipped B-25s (PBJs) to manning lighter-than-air blimps.

The presence of the United States Navy in Pensacola was longstanding, dating back to 1826, when the Warrington Shipyard was built on the site of earlier Spanish ruins. During World War I and immediately afterward, the navy began experimenting with flying boats and, eventually, carrier-based aircraft. The experimentation continued during the 1920s and 1930s. In 1922, Corry Field, named after Lieutenant Commander William M. Corry, was constructed as an auxiliary field for flight training. When this field proved inadequate, a new auxiliary base, Corry Field, was built in 1927, and the original site became an OLF, or outlying field, used primarily for emergency landings or "touch and go's." In August 1940, a larger auxiliary base, Saufley Field, named for Lieutenant R.C. Saufley, naval aviator 14, was added to Pensacola's activities. In October 1941, a third field, Ellyson Field, named after Lieutenant T.G. Ellyson, was commissioned. Another auxiliary field, initially known as Station Field but later named Chevalier Field, was also part of the complex of bases centered on NAS Pensacola. The demand for new pilots grew with America's involvement in the war, and the new auxiliary fields were added. In 1942, Bronson (Tarkiln) Field and Barin Fields were constructed, and Bayou Field, an outlying field from the early 1930s, was used.

Commissioned on July 16, 1943, as an auxiliary to NAS Pensacola, Whiting Field in Milton took its name from Captain Kenneth Whiting, naval aviator 16 and the World War I commander of aviators in combat. Constructed on 2,920 acres of agriculture land, Whiting's complement grew to 3,300 officers and men and 1,431 students. Created from squadrons at both NAAS Saufley Field and NAS Pensacola, the new aviators took up

NAS Pensacola was the original center for naval pilot training. By 1939, however, the number of pilot cadets exceeded the ability of the base to effectively train them, and two additional bases were created to train pilots—one in Corpus Christi, Texas, and the other at NAS Jacksonville. *Courtesy of the Emil Buehler Aviation Museum, NAS Pensacola.*

residence in tents until permanent facilities could be built. Training took place using SNBs, SNJs and PBYs, and WAVES operated Link Trainers to simulate flight conditions. Outlying fields to NAAS Whiting included Choctaw, Holley, Milton and Pensacola Airports.

The training programs at NAS Pensacola and its auxiliary fields were very successful. By war's end in 1945, over 28,000 naval aviators, including 2,775 British and 59 French pilots, had received their wings. By mid-1944, more than 10,000 permanent personnel had been assigned to the bases.

In 1938, the Hepburn Board, headed by Admiral Arthur J. Hepburn, undertook a survey of potential areas of expansion of American naval bases in advance of the United States' involvement in the war. One of the sites surveyed was Camp Foster, the Florida National Guard training base located on the site of Camp Joseph E. Johnston, a World War I base. After negotiations with the State of Florida, Camp Foster was turned over to the navy in exchange for seventy thousand acres in rural Clay County,

NAS Jacksonville, commissioned in September 1940, became a major pilot training base for the navy. More than eleven thousand pilot cadets, along with ten thousand air crewmen, went through rigorous programs to learn to fly such airplanes as the Grumman Avenger. *Courtesy of the Indian River County Historical Society and the Vero Beach Library.*

and the navy was authorized to construct a new pilot training base on April 26, 1939. The residents of Jacksonville and Duval County approved a $1.1 million bond issue to purchase additional land at Black Point, which was then given to the navy. Construction began in late 1939, and the first aircraft landed on the still-unfinished runway on September 7, 1940. The base was officially commissioned one month later on October 15, 1940. By this time, the navy had too many pilot cadets for NAS Pensacola, and many of them were diverted to NAS Jacksonville. From late 1940 until August 1945, more than eleven thousand cadets won their wings at the station, and more than ten thousand air crewmen received training.

Cecil Field, an outlying field of NAS Jacksonville, was constructed on twenty-six hundred acres of land in rural Duval County in June 1941 and eventually served as the final training base for carrier pilots before they were assigned to a theatre of operations. In February 1943, Cecil Field became a Naval Auxiliary Air Station (NAAS). The construction of another outlying field, Whitehouse Field, which consisted of twenty-five hundred acres,

Florida Takes to the Oceans

NAS Mayport opened in 1942 to accommodate ships of the U.S. Navy. This photograph shows the boats and crews lined up at the dock for Saturday morning inspection, circa 1943. *Courtesy of the Beaches Historical Society, Jacksonville Beach.*

NAS Mayport personnel also maintained regular antisubmarine boat patrols to protect against German U-boats prowling the Atlantic. This promotional photograph, taken in 1943, shows two boats returning from a patrol. *Courtesy of the Beaches Historical Society, Jacksonville Beach.*

Lee Field, an auxiliary field for student pilots at NAS Jacksonville, became NAS Green Cove Springs in 1943, and a separate pilot training school was created to rapidly expand the numbers of navy pilots available for use in the Pacific. *Courtesy of the Clay County Historical Society.*

provided enough acreage to handle the demands of the pilot school during the war. Eventually, Cecil Field would grow to more than thirty thousand acres in the postwar period before it closed in 1999.

In 1942, Naval Station Mayport, a port facility, was constructed to accommodate any ship of the navy. Because of its deep-water port, Mayport remained an active naval base after the end of World War II, and currently, Mayport is home to the third largest concentration of ships of the U.S. Navy in the world. In September 1940, Naval Air Station Lee Field opened at nearby Green Cove Springs. In August 1943, the facility was renamed Naval Air Station Green Cove Springs and consisted of four five-thousand-foot asphalt runways and a school for navy fighter pilots.

The Hepburn Board also recommended the construction of a seaplane base on a barrier island along the Indian River Lagoon in Brevard County. Thus, the Banana River Naval Air Station was born. In 1939, a small group of 13 men arrived on the barren beach to begin surveying and laying out the base. On October 1, 1941, some six weeks before the United States entered World War II, the base was formally commissioned as a sub base of NAS Jacksonville. Using PBY Catalinas and PBM Mariners, the navy began antisubmarine patrols along the Florida coast. The PBMs became the principal aircraft used to train new pilots after March 1942 and were replaced on patrol by OS2U Kingfisher seaplanes. Landing strips were constructed in 1943, thereby allowing for concurrent operation of shore-based aircraft. A blimp squadron detachment, an aviation navigation training school and an experimental unit to develop and test instrument landing equipment, Project Baker, were also added over the course of the war. In addition, a large aircraft repair and maintenance facility was located on the base. A small contingent of officers from the Free French Navy was trained as PBM pilots at NAS Banana River. When operational, the base was staffed by over 2,800 officers and men who were responsible for operating some 278 aircraft of various types. The base also employed 587 civilians from the areas.

The work done by the Hepburn Board in 1938 paid dividends immediately after Pearl Harbor. Within a few months, hundreds of new naval bases were

NAS Banana River, built on a barrier island along the Indian River Lagoon, served as an antisubmarine base for seaplanes and as a pilot training base. Pilot trainees learned the intricacies of flying large, amphibious PBYs and PBMs. *Courtesy of the Brevard County Historical Commission.*

Built on a stretch of white sandy beach, Banana River Naval Air Station (circa 1940) offered little in the way of creature comforts for the men and women stationed there. German POWs were used in 1943 to construct a large outdoor swimming pool and other recreational facilities. *Courtesy of the Florida Historical Society.*

established, many of them in the Sunshine State. The earlier funding of municipal airport improvements by the FERA, WPA and other New Deal agencies provided an excellent starting point for building new bases to train the thirty thousand new pilots that the navy estimated would be needed to fight the war in the Pacific. Seven new pilot training bases—at Daytona Beach, Vero Beach, Melbourne, Lake City, Fort Lauderdale, Sanford and DeLand—were established in Florida to supplement the existing training programs at NAS Pensacola, NAS Jacksonville, NAS Miami, NAS Key West and NAS Banana River. The new training bases were expected to be completely operational by August 1, 1942—a goal that was met.

In addition to building new training sites, the navy also expanded and improved its existing facilities to accept the crush of new students in the post–Pearl Harbor period. On September 15, 1942, the navy commissioned NAS Richmond, south of Miami, which became the home of Fleet Airship Group One. This unit was trained to use radar-equipped blimps to provide escort support for naval convoys along the Atlantic coast. Three large hangars, 1,000 feet long, 237 feet wide and 150 feet high, were built out of wood to

This page: Tiny Vero Beach Municipal Airport was acquired by the navy in 1940 and became a vital training base for navy and marine pilots. The base soon expanded to accommodate a large number of training aircraft and antisubmarine patrol aircraft. *Courtesy of the Indian River County Historical Society and the Vero Beach Library.*

house the blimps. At that time, the hangars were the largest wooden buildings in the world and were so voluminous that clouds would occasionally form on the inside and it would rain inside the hangars. Although the hangars were supposed to be fire- and hurricane proof, they were neither, as later events would prove. In September 1945, NAS Richmond was at the center of a category three hurricane. The wooden hangars were severely damaged by the wind and then caught fire and burned to the ground. The damage was so severe that naval authorities decided to close down the base.

Vero Beach city leaders, reading the ominous signs in Europe and the Pacific and seeking to find ways to help the area's unemployed, used workers from the federal Public Works Administration to extend the airport's runways, added permanent lights to make night landings possible and constructed radio and teletype facilities in 1939. In 1940,

A school for WAVES was also established at NAS Vero Beach, and WAVES became an essential part of the training staff at the base. Here the WAVE detachment at the base undergoes an inspection by the base's commanding officer. *Courtesy of the Indian River County Historical Society and the Vero Beach Library.*

Marine and navy pilots were taught the rudiments of dive-bombing at NAS Vero Beach. One of the earliest dive-bombers in service with the U.S. Navy was the Douglas SBD Dauntless, and the plane figured prominently in the U.S. Navy's victory at the Battle of Midway. *Courtesy of the Indian River County Historical Society and the Vero Beach Library.*

the Civilian Aviation Administration (CAA) spent $250,000 to extend the runways again and to construct essential buildings to make it capable of handling military aircraft and personnel. The CAA took the lead in upgrading the airport because the United States was technically neutral in the European conflict.

The earlier planning and preparation for this eventuality made it possible for the navy to take over the airport in early 1942, add fifteen hundred additional acres, formally commission the Naval Air Station Vero Beach in November and quickly begin a training program for marine, WAVES and navy aviators. NAS Vero Beach also had the task of flying regular antisubmarine patrols over the Atlantic. By 1943, some fourteen hundred service personnel and more than 250 aircraft occupied the base. Local residents soon grew used to the cacophony of noise that went on twenty-four hours a day as pilot trainees practiced taking off and landing, while pilots assigned antisubmarine duties regularly did the same. NAS Vero Beach was an essential part of the long line of navy bases that stretched along the Atlantic Coast from Key West to Newfoundland. NAS Vero Beach trainees frequently flew navigation missions to the NAS Banana River (now Patrick Air Force Base) and NAS Melbourne in Brevard County to the north, while NAS Palm Beach and NAS Fort Lauderdale anchored the southern end of the training range. Scattered along this north–south route were several smaller emergency landing fields and bombing ranges. Because of the large number of student pilots at navy and army airfields, and the large number of regular naval personnel who flew antisubmarine missions, the Sunshine State was laughingly referred to as "the world's largest aircraft carrier."

Table 3

NAVAL AIR STATIONS AND AUXILIARY AIR STATIONS IN FLORIDA
1930–1946

CITY	STATION	YEAR COMMISSIONED
Cocoa Beach	NAS Banana River	1940
Daytona Beach	NAS Daytona Beach	1942
	OLF Bunnell	1942
	OLF New Smyrna Beach	1942
	OLF Ormand Beach	1942
	OLF Spruce Creek	1942
DeLand	NAS DeLand	1942
Fort Lauderdale	NAS Fort Lauderdale	1942
Jacksonville	NAS Jacksonville	1939/1940
	NAAS Cecil Field	1940/1943
	NAS Lee Field/Green Cove Springs	1940/1943
Key West	NAS Key West	1940
	NAS Boca Chico	1943

CITY	STATION	YEAR COMMISSIONED
Lake City	NAS Lake City	1942
	OLF Alachua	1942
	OLF Cedar Key	1942
	OLF Gainesville	1942
Melbourne	NAS Melbourne	1942
	OLF Malabar	1942
	OLF Valkaria	1942
Miami	NAS Miami/Opa-Locka	
	NAS Richmond	1942
Pensacola	NAS Pensacola	1826/1935
	NAAS Chevalier	1934
	NAAS Barin Field	1942
	NAAS Bronson	1942
	NAAS Corry Field	1943
	NAAS Ellyson Field	1943
	NAAS Milton/Whiting	1943
	NAAS Saufley Field	1943
Sanford	OLF Osceola	1943
	NAS Sanford	1942
Vero Beach	NAS Vero Beach	1942

Each of the pilot training bases in Florida specialized in teaching students the operations of a particular type of aircraft. NAS Vero Beach, for example, taught marine and navy students the ins and outs of flying navy fighters, such as the F4F Wildcat and the F6F Hellcat, planes that were used primarily in the Pacific War against the Japanese. Marine Night Fighting Group 53, the first such group in the Marine Corps, received its initial training at NAS Vero Beach and went on to train other such units for the corps. To the south of Vero, NAS Fort Lauderdale specialized in the operations of the Grumman TBF Avenger torpedo bomber. To the north at NAS Banana River (now Patrick Air Force Base in Brevard County), students learned to fly PBY and

Two carrier fighters used by the navy were the F4F Wildcat, which had great difficulty against Japanese Zeros, and the F6F Hellcat, which took the Japanese by surprise when it proved more than capable of handling the lightly armored Zero. Because the planes looked almost identical, Japanese pilots often mistook the faster and better-armed Hellcat for the earlier Wildcat, which resulted in a large number of Japanese defeats. *Courtesy of the Indian River County Historical Society and the Vero Beach Library.*

PBM amphibious planes. Elsewhere, Florida bases offered pilot training for bombers, fighters and observation aircraft—virtually every aircraft in the arsenal of the United States.

During 1942, the Merle Fogg Airport in Fort Lauderdale was selected by the United States Navy to be improved into a naval aviation facility for training naval aviators during World War II. The naval aviation training command made NAS Fort Lauderdale into a training facility for naval aviators, supporting aircrew personnel and ground maintenance personnel on the Grumman-designed TBF/TBM Avenger single engine torpedo bomber, a carrier-based airplane.

Training was very strenuous, and eighty student pilots lost their lives from 1942 until 1945. Many instructors were assigned right from aviator training in Pensacola, after being awarded their pilot wings, and so had little practical

NAS Melbourne, formerly the Eau Gallie–Melbourne Municipal Airport, became operational as a pilot training base in October 1942. The base was used to train carrier pilots flying the Wildcat and Hellcat fighters. Shown here is a Hellcat. *Courtesy of the Indian River County Historical Society and the Vero Beach Library.*

experience in the beginning, but some instructors had limited experience in training pilot students, which helped the program greatly in the initial phases. In 1943, Ensign George H.W. Bush, who would later become president of the United States, received his advanced training at NAS Fort Lauderdale.

Naval Air Station Melbourne was commissioned by Rear Admiral Arthur B. Cook on October 20, 1942, on the site of the Eau Gallie–Melbourne Municipal Airport. Like many other civilian airports in Florida, local government officials had used WPA funds to upgrade the airport in 1933. With two outlying fields, Valkaria and Malabar Fields, the navy decided to use the new base to train new carrier pilots in the operation of the F4F Wildcat and the later F6F Hellcat fighters.

With four four-thousand-foot asphalt runways, the base was home to about 150 aircraft of all types, including Stearman trainers and SNJ trainers. With a permanent staff of 1,355 enlisted personnel and 361 officers, the base

Navy WAVES (Women Accepted for Volunteer Emergency Service) operated the LINK simulators that allowed would-be pilots to gain experience before they actually sat in the cockpits of real airplanes. *Courtesy of the Brevard County Historical Commission.*

was also home to a detachment of WAVES who worked in a variety of jobs, including LINK training. The LINK trainer was an early flight simulator that allowed pilots to become familiar with instrument flying without risking either the pilot or a plane. Safety was always a major concern, and despite the best efforts of the training staff to ensure safety, sixty-three pilots died in aerial accidents and an additional two of the station's personnel were killed in ground-related accidents. Not an excessive number of fatalities considering NAS Melbourne produced more than 2,200 new pilots during the course of the war. The base closed on February 15, 1946. It is now the Melbourne International Airport.

NAS DeLand opened in November 1942 on land donated by the City of DeLand. Home to as many as 331 officers and 1,140 enlisted men, the base's principal mission was to provide advanced training for flight crews piloting the PBO Ventura, the PB4Y-2 Privateer and the carrier-based SBD Dauntless bombers. In addition, personnel stationed at NAS DeLand were

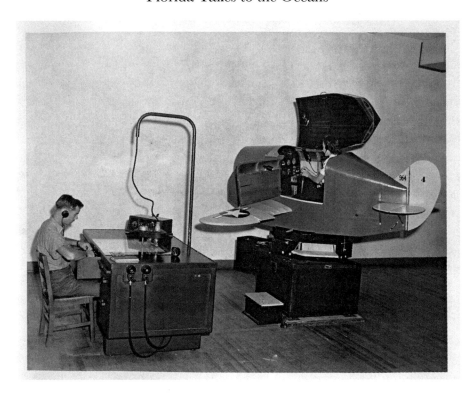

This photograph shows the LINK simulator in operation at NAS Melbourne. Simulated flying was a safe way to give pilot trainees the experience of flying without risking their lives. Sixty-three pilots died in aerial accidents while training at NAS Melbourne. *Courtesy of the Brevard County Historical Commission.*

charged with antisubmarine patrol duties along the Atlantic coast. The base provided a variety of jobs for local civilians, and civic leaders credited navy-paid wages as a major factor in ending the Depression in the city. The base closed in March 1946, and the base property was returned to the city. The former NAS DeLand now serves as the DeLand Municipal Airport.

In December 1942, the navy commissioned the Naval Air Station Lake City on the site of the former Lake City Flying Club. Charged with training navy and marine pilots for the PV-1 Venturas and the PV-2 Harpoons, light bombers that were radar equipped, the base had a complement of 290 officers and 1,150 enlisted personnel. Some 200 WAVES were stationed at the base and performed a variety of tasks as air controllers, meteorologists, aircraft maintenance specialists and administrative specialists. Outlying fields for the naval air station were located in Cedar Key, Alachua and Gainesville.

One month earlier, the navy also opened NAS Sanford with the same mission. Some 1,400 enlisted men, 360 officers and 150 WAVES of all ranks initially conducted training for land-based light bombers and patrol planes. In mid-1944, however, the mission changed to training pilots for carrier-based F4F Wildcats and F6F Hellcats. The base was inactivated in 1946 but was reactivated in 1950 in response to the outbreak of the Korean War.

By the early months of 1942, the U.S. Navy had a major presence on the Florida peninsula, one that would grow through the war years. The primary missions of naval air stations in the Sunshine State were to fly antisubmarine patrols along the coasts to protect Allied shipping and, more importantly, to train more than 100,000 navy and marine pilots for bomber and fighter planes. In addition to its pilot training bases, the navy also used Florida universities as training schools for other critical jobs.

Like the United States Army Air Force, the navy claimed a large portion of Florida skies as its own.

Chapter 7

THE UNITED STATES ARMY IN THE SUNSHINE STATE

Camp Blanding

We are not a warlike people. We have never sought glory as a nation of warriors. We are not interested in aggression. We are not interested—as the dictators are—in looting. We do not covet one square inch of the territory of any other nation. Our vast effort, and the unity of purpose which inspires that effort are due solely to our recognition of the fact that our fundamental rights are threatened by Hitler's violent attempt to rule the world. These rights were established by our forefathers on the field of battle. They have been defended—at great cost but with great success—on the field of battle, here on our own soil, and in foreign lands, and on all the seas all over the world. There has never been a moment in our history when Americans were not ready to stand up as free men and fight for their rights.
—Franklin Delano Roosevelt, September 1941

In June 1939, the United States Army numbered a mere 187,900 men, including the 22,400 members of the Army Air Corps. An additional 200,000 men served in the National Guard units of the various states. In preparation for a war that was almost certain to come for the United States, in August 1940, Congress nationalized the state guards and made them part of the national army. One month later, Congress inaugurated the first peacetime draft for a period of one year. As the war in Europe escalated, Congress lengthened the required service period to "indefinite" in August 1941, just four months before Pearl Harbor. By December 1941, the army numbered 1,685,500 men, of whom 276,000 were in the Army Air Corps (which became the Army Air Forces in June 1941). At the end of the war in 1945, there were more than 8,000,000 men under arms in the United States Army, not counting the 2,400,000 men and women in the Army Air Forces.

To provide training for the millions of new inductees into the army, the War Department quickly began to identify potential new training bases and to upgrade existing ones. In the Sunshine State, Camp Foster, the home of the Florida National Guard, was closed in 1939, and the site was turned over to the navy. In mid-1939, the transaction was complete, and the state armory board chose as compensation a tract of 30,000 acres in Clay County as a National Guard camp and training site. By 1944, the camp encompassed more than 170,000 acres of rural forest and farmlands. More than one million troops would receive all or part of their training at Camp Blanding.

Named after General Albert Hazen Blanding, an 1894 graduate of the East Florida Seminary, the base was leased to the army in November 1940. The army spent more than $28 million constructing the camp, and CCC and WPA workers, as well as local civilians and army personnel, were used to erect permanent and temporary buildings. "If you could hold a hammer,"

Camp Blanding, which would serve as a major infantry-training base, opened in 1939 with nothing but undeveloped forest surrounding Lake Kingsley. A massive construction effort soon saw the erection of ten thousand buildings by 1945. *Courtesy of the Camp Blanding Museum.*

At its peak usage in 1943, Camp Blanding was the fourth largest city in the Sunshine State. More than one million troops received all or part of their army training at the post. *Courtesy of the Camp Blanding Museum.*

said Frank Towers, a ninety-three-year-old volunteer at the Camp Blanding Museum, "you were called a carpenter and put to work." Towers was among the first soldiers to train at the new post.

On the shore of Lake Kingsley, a large sinkhole, the War Department constructed more than ten thousand buildings of all sorts to accommodate the large number of troops that poured into Camp Blanding as the draft got underway. By using soldiers side by side with experienced carpenters, pieces for a simple building, such as a mess hall, could be cut in the lumberyard in a few minutes and erected in less than twenty-five. The influx of new soldiers was so rapid that few permanent barracks were built, and troops were forced to build their own housing. Frank Towers, who was there at the beginning, remembers, "This was a wooden platform about sixteen feet square, with flimsy frame siding with a pyramidal-shaped top, and all covered with what was known as a pyramidal canvas tent. In each one were six double bunks with a small coal stove in the center. This was to be our home for the next year."

An aerial shot of the main headquarters and support buildings at Camp Blanding. The houses at the lower right of the photograph were for the base commander and his staff officers. *Courtesy of the Camp Blanding Museum.*

Trainees lived in tent "hutments" at Camp Blanding. Soldiers, with the help of civilian employees, erected these hutments. *Courtesy of the Camp Blanding Museum.*

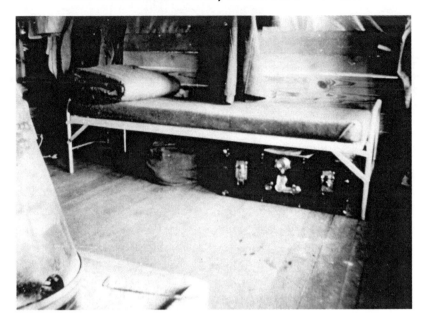

The tent barracks housed six soldiers each. Cots lined the perimeter of the hutments, which featured screened walls and wooden floors. *Courtesy of the Camp Blanding Museum.*

A coal-burning stove occupied the center of each tent. This provided much-appreciated heat during the cold winter months in northern Florida, where temperatures often were below freezing. *Courtesy of the Camp Blanding Museum.*

Outside, the white sand that covered the post was ankle deep, and soldiers were forced to build wooden sidewalks, or "duck-walks," from their quarters to other areas of the company. Construction was always ongoing at Blanding. Some 5,000 civilian workers were hired to complete the camp, and roads leading to the camp were filled with job seekers from the surrounding area and as far north as Alabama, Tennessee and Georgia. Still, the task of building was unceasing, and by early 1942, some 119,000 soldiers were in training at the post—making it the fourth largest city in the Sunshine State. Within a year, Camp Blanding had more than 125.0 miles of paved roads, more than one million square yards of motor parking areas, 81.0 miles of water lines, 26.5 miles of railroad and over 250.0 miles of electrical wiring. In addition, the army was using an advanced artillery range, as well as a variety of specialized ranges for rifle, antiaircraft, mortar and grenade training.

Although the earliest arrivals at Camp Blanding faced formidable challenges, by mid-1943 the post included a number of amenities that led some newspapers to label the camp a "virtual resort." Trainees could take advantage of nine movie theatres, including one outdoor theatre with

CAMP BLANDING, FLORIDA—DRIVER'S PERMIT

Name William W. Braswell   No. **1391**

Sgt. Co. G. 124th Inf.
Rank, Organization, or Civilian Status

Camp Blanding, Fla.
Residence Address

Licensee's Signature Sgt. William W. Braswell

Issued By: L. E. GOODRICH
Colonel, Field Artill

Date MAY 19 1941

Provost Marshal

Eventually encompassing more than 170,000 acres and with more than 125 miles of paved roads, trucks and jeeps were very much in evidence at Camp Blanding, moving men and materiel throughout the post. Army drivers received army licenses after completing a basic safety and driving course. *Courtesy of the Camp Blanding Museum.*

This aerial photograph shows neat lines of tent hutments arranged in company-sized areas at Camp Blanding. Smoke from coal-burning furnaces and stoves envelope the camp, giving it a dull and hazy look. *Courtesy of the Camp Blanding Museum.*

a capacity to seat 5,000 at a time. The remaining eight theatres had a combined seating capacity for 15,700 soldiers. Sports were encouraged, and Blanding boasted a field house with three practice courts, plus a main court for basketball and boxing matches. The eighteen-thousand-square-foot building was large enough to accommodate indoor baseball during periods of inclement weather. Six outdoor tennis courts and eight handball courts, plus a large open beach on Lake Kingsley, provided additional opportunities for sports, to say nothing of the horseshoe, archery and other minor sports courses. Several professional athletes—Babe Ruth, Joe Louis, Bobby Feller, Joe Kirkwood and Ed "Strangler" Lewis—paid visits to Camp Blanding, and Joe Louis brought along a sparring partner to give an exhibition match.

There was a USO in Starke and one on the post to provide "wholesome" entertainment for the troops during their off hours. Cary Grant visited the post in February 1945, and bandmasters Sammy Kaye and Jack Teagarden

With mess kits in hands, troops line up to be fed at their company mess hall at Camp Blanding. Mess halls were among the more permanent buildings on the post, although the anticipated lifetime of such buildings was only ten years. *Courtesy of the Camp Blanding Museum.*

This postcard scene depicts the tent hutments of the soldiers surrounding the company's headquarters and recreation building. Such postcards were sent home by soldiers who wanted their families to see how they lived. *Courtesy of the Camp Blanding Museum.*

staged nationally broadcast dances in the large field house. The 250-woman Women's Army Auxiliary Corps (WAAC, or WAC after August 1943) contingent on Blanding provided a female presence at USO events, which was supplemented by female civilians from the surrounding towns. To ensure that the Blanding soldiers had the opportunity to attend religious services, twenty-eight chaplains staffed twenty-four chapels around the post. Services were offered for Catholics, Jews and Protestants. But even the best efforts of the chaplains and the USO personnel could not keep all of the soldiers on the post, and many eagerly partook of the shadier offerings along the "Boomtown Road."

As important as Camp Blanding was as a military base, it was far more important in changing the surrounding countryside and the small towns in the area when the base was being built. Although it was located mostly in Clay County, Camp Blanding had its greatest impact on nearby Starke, eleven miles west in Bradford County. Green Cove Springs, the county seat of Clay County, thirty or so miles to the east, was home to Lee Field, an auxiliary field for NAS Jacksonville. Lee Field was oriented more to the Jacksonville area and escaped most of the dramatic changes experienced

Girls from surrounding towns, WACs stationed at the base and Red Cross women offered wholesome entertainment and dancing at the USOs at Camp Blanding. Even the Salvation Army had a detachment stationed there. *Courtesy of the Camp Blanding Museum.*

Although Camp Blanding offered a variety of recreational activities on base, most soldiers left the post at every opportunity to explore local towns. These two soldiers, standing on the street corner in downtown Starke, hope to meet some of the local girls. *Courtesy of the Florida State Photographic Archives.*

by Starke, whose population boomed from fifteen hundred to more than twenty-one thousand in just a few months.

In 1979, Rick Cheshire, a journalism student at the University of Florida, described the impact of Camp Blanding for the *Bradford County Telegraph*: "As workers rushed to Camp Blanding, they rushed to Starke. Every spare room in just about every house was rented to the newcomers. Many slept on the street or in cars; some pitched tents in the woods around Blanding."

"Rent jumped from $20–$25 to $50–$60. Land around the camp which had been selling for $15 an acre sold for $15 a front foot," *Time* magazine claimed. In *McCall's* magazine, the author of "Boom Town U.S.A." wrote of two workers, "They were making money all right but both of them had been living in a garage, sleeping there in cots. Each of them paid $10 a week for board and bed."

Although city leaders did their best to cope with the infrastructure changes that the burgeoning population demanded, they were fighting a losing battle. As one writer noted, "Starke had the only chamber of commerce in the state, perhaps the nation, that told people to stay away." Tent cities in vacant fields grew overnight, and any building with a roof could be rented for astronomical sums. When no rooms could be found, workers and their families built shacks out of scrap lumber, empty ammunition boxes and any other materials they could find. Even dilapidated chicken houses and barns were rented. Lumber was scarce; one account says that every piece of lumber in that part of the state "had at least five buyers waiting for it."

Between the gates of Camp Blanding and the Starke city limits, soldiers ran a gauntlet of gambling dens, bordellos and independent prostitutes who prowled the edges of the highway, all wanting a portion of the base's annual payroll of $2.5 million. "'Boomtown Road,'" recalled Frank Towers, "was one prostitute after another, plying their trade in large boxes, small trailers, chicken houses and any other place they could find." Temporary arcades, brightly lit, offered everything from tattoos and quickie photograph booths to food vendors and cheap booze. In the town of Starke, there was no hospital to deal with the virulent outbreak of venereal diseases, broken bones and cuts from bar fights or the daily traffic accidents on the road between the town and the base. Even as city leaders tried to "clean up" the town in the face of Camp Blanding officials' threats to declare it off limits, the problems persisted.

The "good people" of Starke were appalled at the behavior of the workers and soldiers from Blanding. According to the *Bradford County Telegraph*, young women were seldom allowed on the streets of Starke alone; even the USO workers at the camp and in town were picked up by automobile before their shifts and ferried to their jobs. When their shifts were over, they were taken home by car. Noted author Marjorie Kinnan Rawlings, who came to bring a little culture to the Blanding troops, was escorted to and from the base, and Rawlings was not someone easily intimidated. Starke and several smaller towns surrounding it embodied the good and bad aspects of boomtowns of the past—Silver City, San Francisco, Nome—and money flowed through them constantly day and night.

Camp Blanding also had a large hospital that had about twenty-eight hundred beds and was staffed by doctors and nurses permanently assigned to the base. By the end of 1942, almost 2,000 civilians, enlisted men and women and military doctors and nurses performed more than 20,000 in-house procedures. In 1943 alone, more than 750,000 outpatient treatments were made, and from 1943 until the end of 1945, the number of outpatients averaged about 170,000, including on-base and area dependents of military personnel. In 1943, the hospital staff delivered 178 babies in the women's section of the hospital. In 1944, the hospital was designated a Regional Station Hospital and was responsible for treating all military personnel within a seventy-five-mile radius. The standard of care

The base hospital at Camp Blanding was among the largest and best-equipped hospitals in the South. Eventually, the hospital grew to more than twenty-eight hundred beds. *Courtesy of the Camp Blanding Museum.*

108—Station Hospital, Camp Blanding, Fla.

Because of its size and the quality of care provided by the doctors and nurses permanently assigned to the hospital, Camp Blanding became the major treatment facility for army and navy bases throughout the Sunshine State. *Courtesy of the Camp Blanding Museum.*

provided by the hospital staff was so good that it was accredited by the American College of Surgeons.

Some four thousand civilians were hired to perform some of the more traditional jobs on post. Civilians operated the fire department, telephone exchange, water systems and railroad repairs, thus freeing military personnel for training. Thirty-five civilian employees of the U.S. Post Office distributed the mail over the large encampment.

Headquarters Detachment Two, a formation of "colored" troops, was stationed on the base to perform supply, transportation and clerical functions. A second detachment of African American troops, MP Section Two, was also permanently assigned to Camp Blanding and performed routine guard duties, as well as urban patrols in Starke, Green Cove Springs and Jacksonville. These troops occupied a separate bivouac area from that of the exclusively white troops of the divisions that were training. Black troops were also forced to use separate recreational areas and segregated hospital facilities and to sit at the back of military buses, while Camp Blanding's fifteen hundred German and Italian prisoners of war were able to use the same facilities as white soldiers. Dempsey Travis,

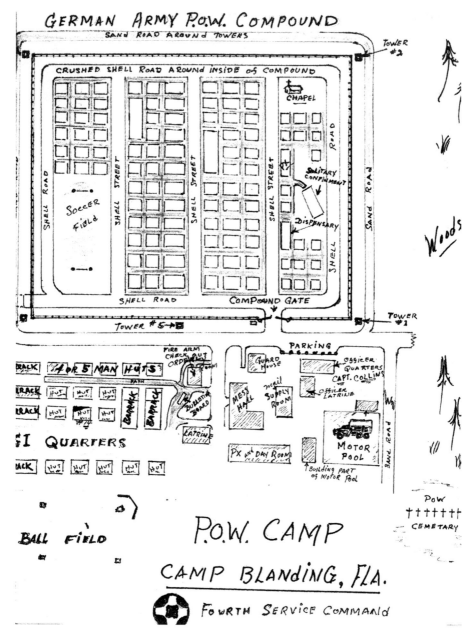

By mid-1943, Camp Blanding was home to 250 German POWs captured in North Africa and Italy. In addition, the post was home to a large contingent of German naval prisoners. Camp Blanding was the major POW base in Florida and operated twenty-two sub camps that held another 2,500 to 5,000 prisoners. This drawing shows the layout of their camp at Blanding. A second, smaller facility was located a short distance away and housed the naval POWs. *Courtesy of the Camp Blanding Museum.*

a noted civil rights activist, author and businessman, noted the same thing during his World War II service:

> *The army was an experience unlike anything I've had in my life. I think of two armies, one black, one white. I saw German prisoners free to move around the camp, unlike black soldiers, who were restricted. The Germans walked right into the doggone places like any white American. We were wearin' the same uniform, but we were excluded.*

The first unit to train at Blanding was the Thirty-first Division, comprising smaller National Guard units from Florida, Louisiana, Mississippi and Alabama, which took up residence in December 1940. In March 1941, the Forty-third Division, made up of smaller units from Maine, Connecticut,

Like all members of the American military, soldiers at Camp Blanding were encouraged to save money through the purchase of war bonds. Large signs were erected around the post to show the progress of each bond drive toward meeting the assigned quotas. *Courtesy of the Camp Blanding Museum.*

Rhode Island and Vermont, joined the Thirty-first at Blanding, which had facilities to accommodate two full divisions at a time. A friendly rivalry developed between the "Dixie Darlings" of the Thirty-first and the Yankees of the Forty-third. These were the first of what would eventually be nine divisions to train at the camp.

When the Thirty-first and Forty-third Divisions departed for other assignments in February 1942, they were quickly replaced by the Thirty-sixth Infantry Division, a National Guard division from Texas, and by the First Infantry Division, the only regular army division to train at Blanding. After a three-month training regimen, the First Division was shipped out, in May 1942, to participate in Operation Torch, the Anglo-American invasion of North Africa, which would come in November. The Thirty-sixth Infantry Division was shipped out in July to another stateside base, but it, too, would end up in North Africa in early 1943.

As quick as one unit was trained, it was relocated, and another took its place at Blanding. Following the departure of the 1st and 36th Divisions,

The infantry troops that trained at Camp Blanding learned to work with field artillery and to coordinate their movements with Allied tanks. This photograph shows a Sherman tank, which was used in great numbers by the United States and its allies. *Courtesy of the Camp Blanding Museum.*

Troops waiting to take their turn on the firing line rest their M-1 Garands on bayonets. Firing ranges for riflemen were only a small part of the specialized ranges and courses built at Camp Blanding. *Courtesy of the Camp Blanding Museum.*

the barracks and tents of the post were quickly filled in August 1942 by men of the 79th Division and the 29th Division, both of which would later participate in Operation Overlord, the Normandy invasion. By mid-1943, three additional divisions—the 30th, the 63rd and the 66th—as well as other specialized units, such as the 508th Parachute Infantry Regiment, several artillery regiments and brigades, a cavalry regiment and several infantry regiments, cycled through Camp Blanding at various times. In July 1943, the focus of training at Blanding shifted from training entire divisions en masse to providing training to individuals who would be replacements for established units in Europe and the Pacific that had lost personnel.

In addition to the nine all-white divisions that trained at Camp Blanding, a substantial number of smaller units utilized the facility as well. Perhaps most noteworthy among these are the Forty-fifth Engineer General Service Regiment (Colored) and the Ninety-seventh Engineer General Service

Regiment (Colored). African Americans, who at the time were segregated from their white counterparts, composed the entirety of each of these units. After their training was finished at Camp Blanding, the men of the Ninety-seventh were assigned to construct parts of the Alaskan-Canadian highway before they shipped out to New Guinea in the Pacific. Upon completion of its Blanding training, the Forty-fifth was shipped overseas to Africa and eventually played a major role in the construction of the Lido Road in India. Incomplete records, however, make it difficult to estimate the exact number of African Americans who trained at Camp Blanding, but the likelihood is that an African American training regiment (or regiments) was stationed at the base after it became an infantry replacement training center in 1943. Unfortunately, the army's records are incomplete, and this cannot be verified.

Trainees who would be transferring to other bases or going on leave were issued a special pamphlet that instructed them on how to utilize army travel vouchers, how to conduct themselves while on trains carrying civilians and how to get assistance from military and civilian authorities if they encountered any difficulties. *Courtesy of the Camp Blanding Museum.*

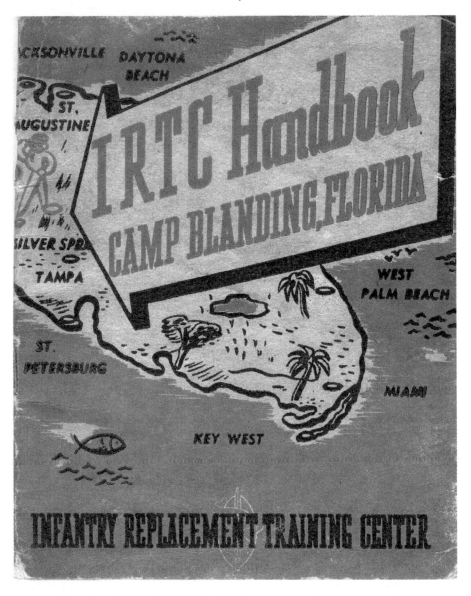

In 1943, Camp Blanding no longer trained divisions en masse but concentrated on training individuals who would be assigned as replacements for army units operating in the European or Pacific theatres. *Courtesy of the Camp Blanding Museum.*

At the end of the war in 1945, Camp Blanding became a center for processing soldiers who were being discharged. As always, the War Department made sure that the soldiers had information they might need. This pamphlet was issued to every soldier leaving the army. *Courtesy of the Camp Blanding Museum.*

Suddenly, however, the boom ended in August 1945, when the Japanese surrendered. By 1946, Camp Blanding had closed temporarily. Starke reverted to its prewar reliance on agriculture, although several small manufacturing concerns did locate there. The 1950 census reported some three thousand residents in the town, a significant increase from the fifteen hundred in 1940 but nothing to compare with the twenty-five thousand reached during World War II.

Camp Blanding remains an active base today, although it is much smaller and less active than it was in the period from 1940 to 1945. A museum, located just outside the main gate in a World War II barracks, preserves the legacy of its beginnings and contributions to the war.

Chapter 8

"Hell by the Sea"

Camp Gordon Johnston

Camp Gordon Johnston was the most miserable Army installation I had seen since my days in Yuma, Arizona, ages past. It had been hacked out of palmetto scrub along a bleak stretch of beach. We were forced to scatter our three infantry regiments miles apart and thus could never train as a complete division. Moreover, it was bitterly cold in that northern leg of Florida. Every training exercise was a numbing experience. The man who selected that site should have been court-martialed for stupidity.
—General Omar Bradley, commanding general, Twenty-eighth Infantry Division, 1983

The outstanding development of this war, in the field of joint undertakings, was the perfection of amphibious operations, the most difficult of all operations in modern warfare. Our success in all such operations, from Normandy to Okinawa, involved huge quantities of specialized equipment, exhaustive study and planning, and thorough training as well as complete integration of all forces, under unified command.
—Fleet Admiral Ernest J. King, chief of naval operations, 1945

In late 1941, the United States Army decided that every theatre of the war would eventually require amphibious landings to breach German and Japanese defenses if America went to war, and plans were made to train American soldiers for this purpose. Initially, the army's amphibious training program was divided between three sites—Camp Edwards, Massachusetts;

Carrabelle, Florida; and Fort Lewis, Washington. Following the Japanese attack on Pearl Harbor and the subsequent declarations of war by the Germans and Italians, the move to train soldiers faster took on a new urgency. The small number of landing craft available for training hampered the effort until early 1943.

In the European theatre of operations, a unified command under the leadership of General Dwight D. Eisenhower made interservice cooperation a reality, and Allied forces in all branches worked together to achieve landings in North Africa, Sicily, Italy and, finally, on the Normandy beaches. In the Pacific theatre, however, an intense rivalry developed between General Douglas MacArthur, who commanded U.S. Army and Army Air Force units, and Admiral Chester W. Nimitz, the commander of naval forces. This rivalry, exacerbated by MacArthur's defeat in the Philippines in 1942 and his

Encompassing more than 155,000 acres of swamps, islands and forests, Camp Gordon Johnston was a temporary training base for amphibious troops. Created in 1942, it was decommissioned in 1945 and bulldozed out of existence in 1946. Only the housing for officers and their families remains, gaining a second life as homes in Lanark Village. *Courtesy of the Camp Gordon Johnston Association Museum.*

massive ego, threatened the success of American military efforts against the Japanese at times. In order to eliminate his dependency on naval personnel to operate the landing craft needed for his campaign of assaulting island strongholds, MacArthur insisted on the accelerated training of soldiers for this job.

In early 1941, the army chose 165,000 acres in rural Franklin County, near the small village of Carrabelle, for this purpose. Originally designated as Camp Carrabelle, the named was changed in early 1942 to Camp Gordon Johnston, in honor of the late Colonel Gordon Johnston, who had received the Medal of Honor for heroism in the Philippine Insurrection of 1906. With MacArthur fighting a defensive fight to protect Australia and Nimitz relying strictly on aircraft carriers to protect Hawaii, no offensive ground operations were possible in the Pacific until enough amphibious landing craft and trained personnel to operate them could be assembled. In May 1942, the War Department ordered the army to begin training twelve divisions in the techniques of amphibious landings and to complete the training by February 1943. A decision was made to make Camp Gordon Johnston the primary training base for all army amphibious operations.

In 1940, Franklin County boasted a population of just over six thousand persons, most of whom were engaged in fishing or timbering. During the first part of the twentieth century, the Georgia, Florida and Alabama Railroad

More than $10 million was spent creating the four smaller camps that made up Camp Gordon Johnston. The largest and most pleasant was the headquarters encampment at Carrabelle. *Courtesy of the Camp Gordon Johnston Association Museum.*

Soldiers training at Camp Gordon Johnston faced a variety of natural dangers in the undeveloped scrublands of the camp. Bears, rattlesnakes and alligators were fierce inhabitants of the area, while millions of mosquitoes were eager to draw blood from the soldiers. *Courtesy of the Camp Gordon Johnston Association Museum.*

touted Franklin County, particularly the Lanark Village area, as a vacation retreat for Georgians. A fashionable hotel, built to house vacationers, burned down in late 1939 and was rebuilt in 1940, just in time to be appropriated by the U.S. Army as living quarters for officers at Camp Gordon Johnston. The decision to build a training base at Carrabelle, which had fewer than one thousand residents in 1940, did not trigger the kind of rush of contractors that Clay and Bradford Counties experienced when construction of Camp Blanding got underway. Although the army spent $10 million to purchase or lease land and to build suitable buildings, the camp remained rough and largely undeveloped throughout its existence.

The first issue of the camp newspaper, the *Amphibian*, appeared on October 16, 1942, and featured a poem by Sergeant Bill Roth that painted a poor picture of Gordon Johnston:

"Hell by the Sea"

The rattlesnake bites you, the horsefly stings,
The mosquito delights you with his buzzin' wings.
Sand burrs cause you to jig and dance
And those who sit down get ants in their pants.

The heat in the summer is one hundred and ten
Too hot for the Devil, too hot for the men.
Come see for yourself and you can tell
It's a helluva place, this Carrabelle.

Although the population of small towns nearby did increase during the war years—Carrabelle's population doubled to about two thousand—overall growth was very small and did not present major infrastructure problems for local authorities. Dependents of soldiers training in the area or stationed there permanently rented every available space in the small towns in the area, which resulted in housing shortages. Like military installations over the world, Camp Gordon Johnston attracted a large number of grifters and prostitutes in the surrounding towns who preyed on unwary soldiers. Local health officials had to deal with steep increases in syphilis and gonorrhea, while law enforcement officers, with the assistance of the military police, worked to keep a damper on crimes and unruliness.

Tallahassee, which was located some sixty miles north, faced the greatest challenge as soldiers from Camp Gordon Johnston clashed with personnel from nearby Dale Mabry Army Airfield. Tallahassee police stayed busy trying to maintain peace between the soldiers. When African American troops, mostly from the North, were sent to Camp Gordon Johnston, the situation became critical when they came face to face with the Jim Crow system of segregation while on passes to Tallahassee, and several riots took place. The mayor of the city asked General William H. Holcombe, the commanding officer at Gordon Johnston, to make the city "off limits" to black troops. Holcombe responded by making the city "off limits" to all soldiers from the post.

Not only were the rough conditions of the camp a shock to the soldiers who were sent there, but also, when they ventured off the post, they encountered cultural shock. In the 1947 history of the 533rd Engineer Boat and Shore Regiment, the author noted, "Carrabelle was dismal proof that *Tobacco Road* was not a figment of its author's imagination." Local residents of the area experienced shock, as well, as the troops at Camp Gordon Johnston flooded the nearby towns while on passes.

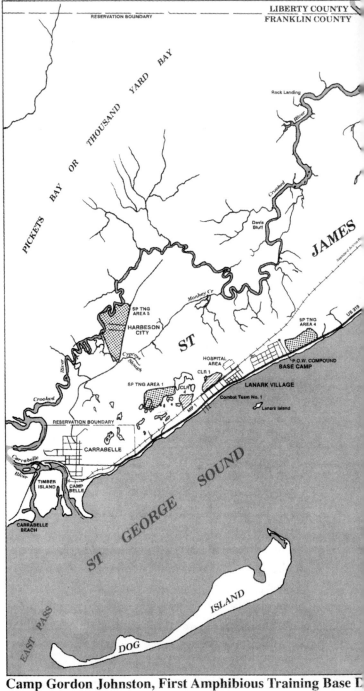

Camp Gordon Johnston occupied the coastline of the Gulf of Mexico from Alligator Point to present-day Carrabelle. Harbeson City, seen near the center of this map, was an abandoned town owned by a timber company that was converted into "Shickelgruber Village," a simulated German village where troops practiced urban warfare skills. *Courtesy of the Florida State Photographic Archives.*

Camp Gordon Johnston, First Amphibious Training Base D

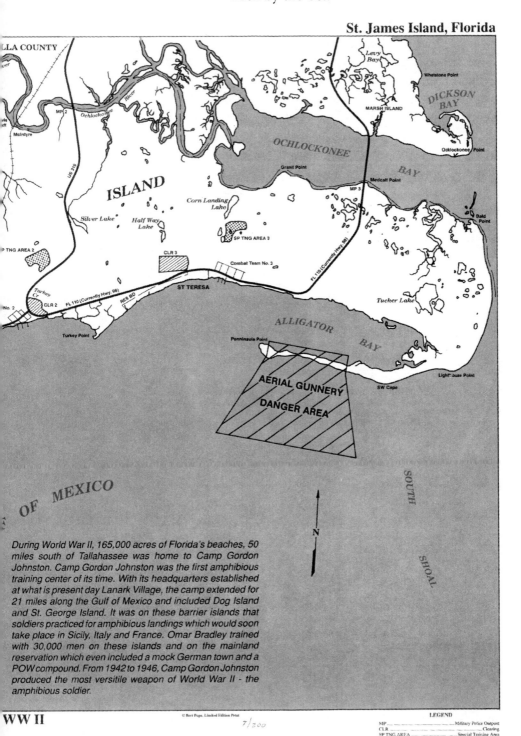

St. James Island, Florida

During World War II, 165,000 acres of Florida's beaches, 50 miles south of Tallahassee was home to Camp Gordon Johnston. Camp Gordon Johnston was the first amphibious training center of its time. With its headquarters established at what is present day Lanark Village, the camp extended for 21 miles along the Gulf of Mexico and included Dog Island and St. George Island. It was on these barrier islands that soldiers practiced for amphibious landings which would soon take place in Sicily, Italy and France. Omar Bradley trained with 30,000 men on these islands and on the mainland reservation which even included a mock German town and a POW compound. From 1942 to 1946, Camp Gordon Johnston produced the most versitile weapon of World War II - the amphibious soldier.

WW II

© Bert Pope, Limited Edition Print

7/300

LEGEND

MP	Military Police Outpost
CLR	Clearing
SP TNG AREA	Special Training Area
	Reservation Boundary
SP TNG AREA, NO. 5	Mock German Town

Camp Gordon Johnston, referred to as "Hell by the Sea" or "Alcatraz by the Sea," had a large land area of swampy, snake-infested, subtropical jungle surrounded by rolling sandy hills, which bordered equally swampy beaches and mangrove swamps on the Gulf of Mexico. Very little physical preparation had been done on the base, and the first job of the permanent training personnel was to clear areas for tent barracks and teaching areas. In addition, docks, maintenance facilities and the normal buildings for support—mess halls, a hospital, permanent barracks, post exchanges, latrines—had to be built. Infrastructure construction was an ongoing effort, as sewers, roads, electrical

This aerial view of the main base at Camp Gordon Johnston shows the beaches and docks where practice landing craft were stored. It also vividly depicts how sparsely developed the base was. *Courtesy of the Camp Gordon Johnston Association Museum.*

The beaches and bays at Camp Gordon Johnston were used to teach the techniques of amphibious landings to army troops. This photograph shows soldiers disembarking from a Higgins boat with its hinged front. Unfortunately, one accident happened at Camp Gordon Johnston when troops were disembarked too far from the shore and became trapped under the front of the boat. Fourteen soldiers drowned under the weight of their gear, a circumstance that would be repeated in numerous real combat landings. *Courtesy of the Camp Gordon Johnston Association Museum.*

generators and telephone systems were absolutely essential. The overall plan called for the camp to be divided into four separate areas. Three areas, home to combat regimental teams, would be located on the beaches, while a fourth area would be located farther inland. The beaches would be home to the troops undergoing training, and the fourth area was reserved for administrative purposes and permanent personnel.

Joe Sullivan, a soldier in one of the training units at Camp Gordon Johnston, recalled how desolate the base was:

I was a member of Company C and arrived at Camp Gordon Johnston, Florida, from Cape Cod, Massachusetts on 9 September, 1943. I was eighteen years old with only two months of service. We trained as

Barbed wire fences, hidden traps and dragon's teeth were just a few of the obstacles soldiers faced once they landed on Camp Gordon Johnston's beaches. Training cadre tried to duplicate obstacles that Allied intelligence units had identified on enemy beaches. *Courtesy of the Camp Gordon Johnston Association Museum.*

combat engineers and then went to manning landing craft. There we trained the 4th Infantry Division in Amphibian warfare. Then the New Years holidays arrived.

With nothing to do and nowhere to go, we were restricted to the Camp and the small town of Carabelle [sic], *Florida. It was decided that we would have a New Years Eve booze party, and a volunteer was asked to go into Carabelle, secure liquor, evade detection by the MP's at the Camp gate and return to the Company area. This sounded to me like more fun than I had in months of boring army training. A challenge to defy authority! I went for it.*

Everyone chipped in, and my buddy and I hitched a ride into Carabelle at sunset. We walked the boardwalk to the nearest liquor store. We bought about twelve bottles of liquor and a large bottle of Champagne for myself. I spotted a large Packard sedan taxi with the spare tires mounted on each side of the car body. We made a deal with the cabby. First we pulled off the tires, stashed the tubes and stored the bottles in the remounted tires, and off we went, back to Camp.

Arriving at the well-lit front gate of Camp Gordon Johnston, we found that it was manned by two MP's and their commander, a 2nd Lieutenant. We were ordered "OUT OF THE CAR!" These guys must have been tipped off because they pulled out all the car seats, opened and searched the trunk, searched under the hood and even crawled under the car, but they did not pull off the two spare tires. Sitting beside the 2nd Lt. was a cluster of confiscated bottles which I'm sure were headed for the "O" club (Officer's Club) that night. After the exhausting search of the car, off we went to the best all-male party ever at Camp Gordon Johnston. Having no ice to cool my wine, I ended up at the back door of the "O" club and got myself a bucket of ice. We screwed the system and had a wonderful time.

Despite the rough conditions of the camp, soldiers who were stationed there permanently or who cycled through the training programs retained fond memories of Camp Gordon Johnston. Each year, Carrabelle hosts a reunion of these "veterans of Hell by the Sea"; they visit the local museum dedicated to the camp and share stories of their adventures.

While each unit cycled through Camp Gordon Johnston at a rapid two-month pace, the men acquired a number of critical skills. From removing beach obstacles to night operations and commando training, the training went on day and night. One of the most remarkable features of the program was to use an abandoned logging village, Harbeson City, to simulate a European village. Troops were taught to fight house to house, much like the kind of fighting they would encounter in European towns and villages. Live ammunition and large amounts of explosives added a realistic flavor to the training. Soldiers were taught how to deal with booby traps, how to search houses and how to fight in the narrow confines of urban streets. Two days of instruction were given to each infantry battalion, during which time each platoon solved a tactical problem in the village using live ammunition.

Although more than 250,000 troops went through amphibious training there, the future of Camp Gordon Johnston was always in doubt. As soon as it was established and training began, the struggle between the army and the navy went on. On November 5, 1942, just months after the camp opened, General Lesley McNair, the commanding general of the U.S. Army Ground Forces in charge of all training programs, recommended that the army

"Ducks" were amphibious wheeled vehicles that were used to ferry men and materiel from ships to shore. The term "Duck" came from the formal designation—DUKW (D=1942, U=amphibian, K=front-wheel drive, W=rear-wheel drive)—given to the vehicle by the military. Soldiers at Camp Blanding became familiar with the vehicles, which were used in virtually all amphibious landings in the war. *Courtesy of the Camp Gordon Johnston Association Museum.*

Barrage balloons were used to protect troops in Ducks and Higgins boats from aerial attacks and from bombing while they were landing. Troops training at Camp Gordon Johnston were often accompanied on their field exercises by balloon units. *Courtesy of the Camp Gordon Johnston Association Museum.*

"Hell by the Sea"

Beach obstacles and realistic explosions, directed by Camp Gordon Johnston's training cadre, were part of the landing exercises practiced by troops at the base. *Courtesy of the Camp Gordon Johnston Association Museum.*

continue conducting amphibious training, but if the navy wanted to assume full responsibility for that program the army would abandon Camp Gordon Johnston and turn the entire base over to it. He reiterated his recommendation on November 9. In January 1943, he notified General Frank A. Keating, who had overall responsibility for amphibious training in the army, "We have decided, as you probably know, that your plant will operate independently and irrespective of what the Navy may or may not do." That bold affirmative statement was reversed just two months later when the army chief of staff, the chief of naval operations and the commander in chief of the U.S. fleet reached an agreement to discontinue the training for army units, with the exception of two brigades assigned to Douglas MacArthur in the Pacific. The official end to the ambitious army amphibious program came on June 10, 1943, although the effective termination date had been in mid-March. Amphibious training now became the sole responsibility of the navy at bases in Norfolk and Camp Bradford, Virginia, and Fort Pierce, Florida.

The training staff and headquarters personnel were transferred to newly activated divisions, assigned to replacement depots to fill the manpower

Troops at Camp Gordon Johnston practice shooting their antiaircraft guns at targets high overhead. This was part of the effort to make training programs as realistic as possible. *Courtesy of the Camp Gordon Johnston Association Museum.*

A platoon leader maintains shore-to-ship contact with supporting naval vessels during this landing exercise in 1943. *Courtesy of the Camp Gordon Johnston Association Museum.*

needs of established divisions or sent to other service schools. A few were assigned to work with navy amphibious training programs. The men of the Seventy-fifth Composite Infantry Training Battalion were reassigned to Camp Pickett, Virginia, for duty as demonstration troops for the Amphibious Training Command, U.S. Atlantic Fleet. In December 1943, this battalion was disbanded, which ended the army's efforts to train amphibious troops.

What became of Camp Gordon Johnston? When amphibious training was turned over to the navy in 1943, the camp was given new responsibilities for training support units for ship-to-shore communications and heavy weapons-air support coordination between ships, ground troops and planes. In addition to providing basic training for new soldiers and training for boat crews and amphibious truck operators, during this time more than

Soldiers line up to get chow at one of the outdoor mess halls at Camp Gordon Johnston. Conditions at the post remained primitive throughout its existence. Only a few permanent buildings were erected, including kitchens, which were necessary to keep blowing sand from contaminating the food that was being prepared. *Courtesy of the Camp Gordon Johnston Association Museum.*

Chaplains conducted religious services outdoors at Camp Gordon Johnston. A base chapel was built at the main headquarters encampment, but most of the troops were located in temporary camps miles away. *Courtesy of the Camp Gordon Johnston Association Museum.*

thirteen hundred African American troops were stationed at Camp Gordon Johnston. Eventually, a portion of the camp, Alligator Point, was used as a gunnery range for fighter aircraft from Dale Mabry Field.

In March 1944, Camp Gordon Johnston received its first batch of 250 German and Italian POWs, who were put to work improving the base facilities. Originally a sub camp that received its prisoners from the larger camp in Aliceville, Alabama, Camp Gordon Johnston was eventually made a base camp on May 1, 1944. It had three outlying sub camps—Dale Mabry Field in Tallahassee, Eglin Field and Telogia, ninety-seven miles west of Camp Gordon Johnston. Prisoners at Dale Mabry and Eglin performed necessary labor on the military bases, but the labor of the prisoners at Telogia was contracted by private industry to supply timber and pulpwood. By the end of 1944, Camp Gordon Johnston was home to about 500 POWs.

Conditions for prisoners at Camp Gordon Johnston were primitive—tents housing five to six men, a canteen in a tent, a mess hall, no flushing toilets and no recreation facilities—but they were little different from those endured by members of the U.S. military. Although conditions improved somewhat, they were never equal to those provided to prisoners at Camp Blanding. By mid-1946, the POW camp was shut down, and the inmates were transferred to other camps in the United States to await repatriation to Germany.

The surrender of the Japanese in August 1945 ended the need for Camp Gordon Johnston, and the camp underwent a gradual closure. Leased land was returned to its original owners, and property purchased by the army was put up for sale. The few structures worthy of saving passed into private hands, but most were simply bulldozed. Camp Gordon Johnston officially closed in March 1946, and by the end of that year, little remained of this base, once the largest in Florida. Little, that is, except the memories of the soldiers and prisoners who spent time at "Hell by the Sea" in Franklin County, Florida.

A WAC detachment stationed at Camp Gordon Johnston leads a parade down the street of nearby Carrabelle. Unlike Starke, near Camp Blanding, Carrabelle did not experience a population explosion, largely because the troops that trained at the base were usually there for a short period of two to three months. *Courtesy of the Camp Gordon Johnston Association Museum.*

Although it was a small town, Carrabelle had its volunteers. In this photograph, female volunteers for the local Red Cross chapter roll bandages for use by American military forces. *Courtesy of the Camp Gordon Johnston Association Museum.*

Table 4
UNITS STATIONED AT CAMP GORDON JOHNSTON
1942–1945

PERMANENT UNITS
HQ & HQ Company, 3rd ESB
HQ Medical Detachment
PERMANENT UNITS
1061st Port Construction and Repair Group
1463rd Engineer Maintenance
563rd Engineer Boat Maintenance

375th Transportation Corps Harbor Craft
22nd Infantry, 4th Infantry Division
105th Harbor Craft Training Reg. & Coast Guard Detachment
332nd, 339th, 344th, 353rd, 356th, 376th, 377th Harbor Craft Companies
534th, 544th, 593rd, 584th EB & SR
3rd Engineer Special Brigade
1st Engineer Amphibian Brigade
534th Scouts
351st, 5th Platoon
75th Composite Infantry Training Battalion
SMALL UNITS
377th Coast Artillery Battalion
6th Communication Squadron
7th Communication Squadron
2nd Chemical Battalion
3rd Chemical Battalion
79th Smoke Generator Company
DIVISIONS
4th Infantry Division
28th Infantry Division
38th Infantry Division

Chapter 9

ROSIE THE RIVETER

War on the Homefront

"Welder"
Slowly upon the ways the gray ships rise,
The hammers ring on forepeak, hold and keel.
Under our gloved hands and hooded eyes,
The blue arc stitches up the patterned steel.
Over the hulls, between the clanging cranes,
We climb and kneel and seam the ships together,
Women are always sewing for their men,
It tides the heart through many a bitter weather.
The chattering rivets button up the shell,
The waiting bay is laced with windy foam,
The molten stitches glow beneath my hand,
This is the ship on which he may come home.
—*Irene Carlisle,* Saturday Evening Post, *February 3, 1945*

Between 1942 and 1945, some five million women entered the American workplace for the first time. These new employees added to the roughly twelve million women already employed in various jobs. War industries, however, afforded women opportunities to enter new areas of work and to move from low-paying, mundane jobs into positions that paid better and allowed them to take on more responsibility. White women, in particular, were welcomed as workers. Women joined the workforces of shipyards and other defense industries within a few months of the declaration of war. Although the initial groups of women were used in office positions or in "soft" jobs like drafting or driving, this quickly changed as manpower became scarcer. During World War II, the percentage of American women who worked outside the home at paying jobs increased from 25 to 36 percent. More married women, more mothers and more minority women found jobs than had them before the war. Mary Anderson, the head of the Women's Bureau of the Department of Labor, summed up the new role of women: "Almost overnight, women were reclassified by industrialists from a marginal to a basic labor supply for munitions making."

While some female workers were quick to admit that "women aren't naturally mechanically inclined," they nonetheless insisted that they were "equally as capable as men," and as the need for additional laborers became more acute, women moved out of the offices and into the yards and onto the assembly lines. Shipyards in Florida found women to be good workers who demonstrated their capabilities every day. In Tampa, for example, the *Tampa Tribune* published an article on the contributions of female workers at the TASCO yard in June 1942. One month later, the *Tribune* featured a front-page story about Alma Brown, the first female welder at the yard, noting the fact that "the ultra-conservative local No. 432 of the Boilermakers' union, as hard-boiled an outfit as ever pushed a ship into the sea" had just approved her membership. Brown, who had completed a ten-week welding course at a local vocational school and had entered the yard as a probationary trainee, was initially viewed skeptically by her male co-workers. Nevertheless, her supervisor told the *Tribune*, "[I'm] sure, she'll get along all right. She's a little bit of a curiosity now to the boys, but when we get five or six more the curiosity will wear off." Her admission into the Boilermakers came weeks before the national leadership submitted the issue to a vote from the general membership. In this way, the sixty-two-year-old prohibition against female members fell by the wayside, and the union leadership found itself rushing to keep pace with its locals.

By 1943, female welders had become so commonplace in both the TASCO and Hooker's Point yards that they received little extra attention. By 1944, enough women were employed in the Hooker's Point facility that the company could hold a yard-wide contest to select the best female welder and sponsor her in competition with other yards operating in the

Female workers operate the switchboard at the busy Wainwright Yards in Panama City. Women filled traditional roles during the war but also took on hundreds more that they had not done before. *Courtesy of the Bay County Library*.

eastern United States. Fully 20 percent of all workers in Tampa shipyards were women by mid-1943, and what happened in Tampa was repeated over and over again in other Florida shipyards, as well as in other kinds of war industries. Over 200,000 women worked in the shipyards of America, and women made up almost 50 percent of the workers in the nation's aircraft factories. Though women did get into a greater array of industrial jobs, they were more likely to be in such lesser-skilled jobs as welding than in riveting. However, some filled highly technical jobs such as patternmaking and electronics assemblies, where their manual dexterity was often greater than that of their male co-workers. Women filled the offices of companies engaged in war work, performing clerical and secretarial jobs—positions they often retained in the postwar period. By war's end, some 2.5 million more women worked in blue-collar jobs in 1944 than had in 1940, and they performed a greater range of jobs than ever before.

In 1942, Redd Evans and John Jacob Loeb, songwriters for the Paramount Music Company in New York, published their pacan to female workers: Rosie the Riveter. An opening voice informs listeners, "While other girls attend their fav'rite bar, sipping dry Martinis, munching caviar, there's a girl who's really putting them to shame [and] Rosie is her name." On May 29, 1943, the *Saturday Evening Post* added to the fame of female war industries workers when it published a well-muscled, idealized portrait of Rosie by Norman Rockwell on its cover. Seated comfortably on a pier piling, eating a sandwich with her rivet gun resting in her lap, she rests her feet on a copy of Adolph Hitler's *Mein Kampf*. The look of confidence on her face said it all: "I'm confident and competent. I'm doing my bit to win this war." Rosie took on many personalities—and other names, like Wanda the Welder and Betty Builder, although Rosie was the most popular—and appeared on countless posters urging more work. With her fist defiantly raised, her shirtsleeves rolled up and a steely look in her eyes, she was the "asexual warrior of the homefront." True, the posters carefully portrayed a certain degree of femininity but little of an overtly sexual nature. The Rockwell portrait presents Rosie as a very masculine figure with bulging muscles and broad shoulders.

One of the most important changes for females in the workplace was the entry of married women in greater numbers. This was particularly true of older women with few or no responsibilities for young children. By 1945, married women over thirty-five made up the majority of females in the labor force of the United States. Younger women with children under six years of age accounted for only 12 percent of America's workforce, an increase of only 3 percent from the prewar years. In Great Britain, Russia and Canada, women were also essential to war production, and their work freed millions of men to become members of the armed forces. Even without a uniform, the contributions of women in the workplace made ultimate victory possible.

Not all women worked in war industries. With a significant portion of American males entering the armed services, women stepped in to fill the vacancies they left behind. Women became bank tellers, plumbers, roofers, bus drivers, taxi operators and salespersons and filled hundreds of other professions. The infusion of additional women into the workforce ensured that American society would maintain a certain normality, despite the manpower demands of the military. Although the war resulted in increased opportunities for women in the workplace, manufacturers continued to take advantage of their supposed inferiority as workers and paid them only 65 percent (on average) of the wages they paid to men in identical positions.

137BUPL=ISEPT44=626-2=OPERATIONS DEPT

Civilian women worked alongside military personnel in order to keep operations going. This is a photograph of the Operations Department at Hendricks AAF in Sebring. *Courtesy of the Sebring Historical Society.*

Not all women entered the workforce voluntarily. For many women, working outside the home was an economic necessity to supplement low family incomes. Approximately 17 percent of all families in the United States were headed by women in 1941, and government subsidies did not pay enough to cover the costs of housing, feeding and clothing these families. This problem was not limited to single women, and wives of servicemen often took jobs to supplement the small allotment checks they received from the military. Standard allotment rates were fifty dollars a month for wives and twenty dollars for each child in the family—important income, but not enough to cover basic living costs.

Traditional family structures underwent changes for some families. As married women entered the workplace, finding suitable childcare for smaller children often meant moving into the homes of parents or in-laws or bringing older relatives into the home. Some enterprising women merged families to allow each mother to have live-in day-care while working different

In order to encourage workers, particularly women, to take jobs, companies like Hooker's Point Shipyard in Tampa and Wainwright Shipyard in Panama City provided housing for them at a reasonable rent rate. This is a photograph of a Wainwright worker's house in Panama City that is still in use today. *Courtesy of the Bay County Library.*

shifts. Social commentators bemoaned the generation of latchkey kids, who were left alone while their mothers went to work. Innovative employers, recognizing the concerns of mothers, often built child-care facilities at plants or paid for such facilities at company housing units. In Tampa, the Maritime Commission constructed six hundred housing units for workers at the new Hooker's Point facility adjacent to the yard. The project, known as Maritime Homes, included a grocery store, beauty shop, barbershop, day-care center and theatre.

The need for an organized child-care program became apparent very early as the United States geared up for war. In 1941, Congress approved the Community Facilities Act, which created child-care centers for children whose parents worked in war production areas. The federal government provided 50 percent of the funds needed to operate the centers; states, localities and parents provided the remaining 50 percent in matching funds. In 1943, the cost to parents for childcare in one of these centers was uniformly set at fifty cents a day. Reaction to these federally financed centers varied from area to area and family to family. Some parents refused to place their children in the care of "strangers," and some local politicians refused to make use of the program because "it meant the state was in the business of raising children." Nevertheless, some 129,000 children did participate in this program nationwide.

President Franklin Delano Roosevelt recognized the importance of female workers in his State of the Union address on January 6, 1942 (and in his addresses in 1943 and 1944), when he said:

> *Production for war is based on men* and women—*the human hands and brains which collectively we call Labor. Our workers stand ready to work long hours; to turn out more in a day's work; to keep the wheels turning and the fires burning twenty-four hours a day, and seven days a week. They realize well that on the speed and efficiency of their work depend the lives of their sons and their brothers on the fighting fronts.*

Female workers can be found among this gathering of workers at a war bond rally at the American Machinery Company factory in Casselberry. Women worked in a variety of jobs for the AMC in its different factories. *Courtesy of the Orange County Regional History Center.*

In the Axis bloc—Germany, Italy and Japan—women were less of a force in war production. Germany relied primarily on male workers, augmented by slave labor and workers from conquered countries, who were impressed into the workforce. Only toward the end of the war did German women become a significant presence in factories. Italian and Japanese women played few roles in industrial production and remained largely uninvolved in the war efforts of their respective countries. Axis production of critical war materiel never matched the output of the Allied countries and this failure materially affected the outcome of the war.

Hundreds of thousands of other women did not enter the workplace, but they also contributed on a volunteer basis. In most cities and towns, volunteer women staffed Red Cross offices, USOs and traveler's aid kiosks in train and bus stations; rolled bandages; collected food parcels to be sent to soldiers; chaperoned dances; volunteered in hospitals; and undertook myriad other tasks to assist the war effort. The USO was a particular favorite of FDR's, and he served as its first honorary chairman. In mid-1940, he proposed that six prominent aid organizations—the YMCA, YWCA, National Catholic Community Service, the National Jewish Welfare Board, the Traveler's Aid Association and the Salvation Army—come together to handle the on-leave and recreational needs of members of the American armed forces, which had increased dramatically because of the draft. By 1944, more than three thousand USOs, staffed by mostly female volunteers, operated throughout the United States and overseas.

Popular female movie stars, singers and other performers contributed their time and energy by visiting stateside hospitals or by becoming spokespersons for bond drives. Well-known entertainer and comedian Bob Hope led several USO tours overseas near the frontlines, and he was always accompanied by famous actors, actresses and dancers or by young starlets seeking to make a name for themselves. He was awarded a congressional Gold Medal for his contributions to winning the war, and he continued to make appearances in front of troops—along with a retinue of young women and seasoned female performers—until just a few years before his death. USO shows during World War II played within a few miles of enemy forces and sometimes were shelled during their performances.

Women, particularly those who were nurses, were also asked to volunteer for military service. The need for nurses to staff hospitals was so great that President Roosevelt proposed in his State of the Union address on January 6, 1945, that twenty thousand qualified women be drafted to bring the number of nurses to sixty thousand. Although Congress failed to act on this

Draftees and volunteers left daily from bus stations and railroad terminals like Union Station in Tampa. Families and first-time travelers often needed assistance, and female volunteers were often in attendance to provide it. *Courtesy of the Hampton Dunn Collection, University of South Florida Special Collections.*

Left: This unidentified Red Cross worker was a paid worker at Camp Blanding. Social service work was one of the new professions that women were hired to fill. *Courtesy of the Camp Blanding Museum.*

Below: Unidentified young women provide companionship to soldiers from MacDill AAF at the USO in Tampa. Some young women worked regular shifts in local defense industries and volunteered at the USO and other social agencies. *Courtesy of the Hampton Dunn Collection, University of South Florida Special Collections.*

Francis Langford, a native of Lakeland, Florida, was a popular singer on the Bob Hope radio program. She frequently joined him on USO tours in Europe and the Pacific. Her last USO trip with Bob Hope came in 1989 when they visited the Persian Gulf. *Courtesy of the Florida State Photographic Archives.*

recommendation before the end of the war, the request reflects how critical women had become to the war effort.

Propaganda campaigns urging women to take an active role in the war effort were frequent. Women who chose to stay at home were told that little

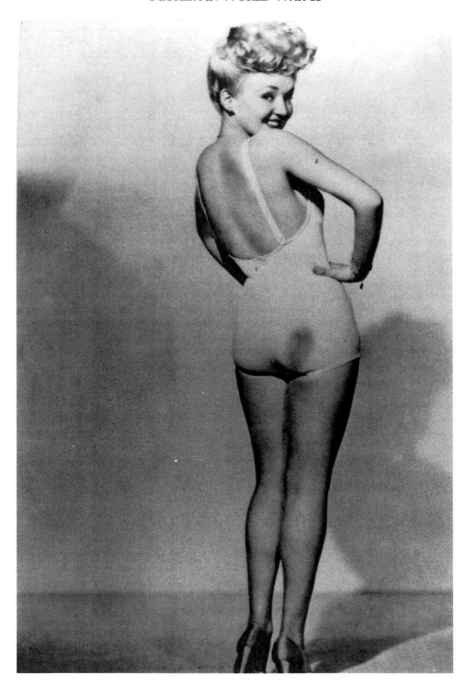

Popular pinup Betty Grable often took part in USO tours between pictures. USO visits by media stars boosted morale and provided entertainment to troops overseas. It was common for these stars to visit injured or sick soldiers in hospitals, a tradition that continues today. *Courtesy of the Camp Blanding Museum.*

things—like walking to do their shopping, planting a victory garden, planning menus around the idea of "meatless" days and even recycling and repairing clothing instead of buying new items—mattered to the overall success of America's war effort. Victory gardens significantly increased available food supplies for the American public at the same time as they promoted a sense of participation in winning the war. Large and small, ranging in size from small urban plots to large suburban and rural fields, over twenty million victory gardens were planted by 1943, and one government official estimated that they produced more than one-third of all vegetables grown that year.

Stay-at-home women were encouraged to open their homes to provide day-care services for the children of women who had taken jobs and other small tasks that would relieve the stress on married women in the workplace. Traditional family structures were altered when husbands went off to war and married women became single parents responsible for raising children alone. American families were increasing by large numbers. The marriage rate (per 1,000 unmarried women aged fifteen and over) rose from 73 in 1939 to 93.6 in 1942 before declining to 84.5 in 1945. Sadly, many wartime marriages were hasty and did not survive long military separations. As a result, divorces soared, going from 25,000 in 1939 to 359,000 in 1943 and 485,000 in 1945.

The annual birth rate per 1,000 people, which had been 18.4 in 1933, rose to 19.4 by 1940 and shot up to 22.7 by 1943. The rate of babies born to unmarried women increased by 42 percent from 1939 to 1945. The dramatic increases in marriage and birth rates can be attributed to several things. Certainly, the increasing prosperity brought about by the New Deal and the outbreak of war made it easier for young couples to get married. With the implementation of the draft in 1940, marriage increased as young men sought exemptions from being called—an increase that was mirrored in 1942 when marriage exemptions were limited to married men with children. One popular joke of the period centered on a new baby named "Weatherstrip," so called because he kept his father "out of the draft."

Women proved themselves capable of dealing with the burdens of working in war industries, of raising children without the presence of a male figure in the family and of handling the day-to-day problems of family life. They also proved to be a vital component in the ultimate victory of the United States and its allies. The gains made in the workplace would be hard to surrender in the postwar period, and although some women willingly gave up working to return to being housewives, others did not.

As late as October 21, 1944, the *Pensacola Press Journal* editors still embraced the idea that the genie of female workers could be placed back in the bottle once the war ended. "When victory is won," they wrote, "all these women will come back home again and settle down to do the work God intended—to comfort and sustain husbands…and to train their sons and daughters in the principles that will make war forever unnecessary." How wrong they were.

Chapter 10

PROSTITUTES, VICTORY GIRLS AND VENEREAL DISEASES

Social Problems

"For Honour and for Her!"
Somewhere a woman, thrusting fear away,
Faces the future bravely for your sake;
Toils from dawn to dark; from day to day,
Fights back her tears, nor heeds the bitter ache;
She loves you, trusts you, breathes in prayer your name.
Soil not her faith in you, by sin or shame.
Somewhere a woman, Mother, Sweetheart, Wife,
Waits betwixt hopes, and fears for your return;
Her kiss, her words, will cheer you in the strife,
When death confronts you grim and stern.
But let her image all your reverence claim,
When base temptations scorch you with their flame.
Somewhere a woman watches filled with pride,
Shrined in her heart you share a place with none;
She toils, she waits, she prays, till side by side,
You stand together when the battle's done.
O, keep, for her dear sake a stainless name,
Bring back to her a manhood free from shame.
—Margaret Scruton, 1939

There were some women who exerted a less-than-positive influence on the war effort. Frequently referred to by disparaging names like "victory girls," "khaki-wackies," "good-time girls," "pick-ups," "good-time Charlottes" or "patriotutes," these women added a sexual dimension to the war. They were a curious mixture of hardened professionals, idealistic amateurs and lonely wives and widows, and sometimes they included women working in war industries.

Who were the victory girls? In her 1981 book, *Wartime Women,* Karen Anderson stated that the general assumption was that she was a young woman who actively sought out the company of servicemen and viewed sex with them as her contribution to the war effort. Authorities usually distinguished between victory girls and professional prostitutes, since for many of the former young ladies the only payment received was the price of a Coca-Cola at the local soda fountain, the price of admission to the movies or a meal at a local restaurant. Newspapers of the period generally reported that victory girls were "country girl[s] who come to town and get into bad company." Victory girls were also young women who, without actually engaging in sexual relations, explored the boundaries of social freedom in wartime America. One study of women arrested and charged with "immorality" during the war years reported that many were young married women. Another study notes that delinquency rates for females below the age of twenty-one increased dramatically between 1940 and 1945, a trend that can only be partially explained by the induction of young males into military service.

Not all victory girls were unmarried and naïve. Some were married women or widows, older and more experienced. The number of marriages also increased significantly during the war years as teenage girls married their high school sweethearts as soon as they received their draft notices. Many of these young brides followed their young husbands to rural towns situated near training bases, hoping to create some semblance of a normal marriage. Often forced to live in substandard housing and seldom seeing their mates, these women were at loose ends. When their husbands were shipped overseas, many of the girl-brides remained near the bases or migrated to war industries in larger towns and cities. Inexperienced, vulnerable and freed from the restrictions of watchful parents or relatives, they often sought to fill the lonely days and nights by frequenting places where other servicemen congregated.

Prostitutes, Victory Girls and Venereal Diseases

Women of all ages, even those participating in volunteer activities such as the USO, were susceptible to giving in to romantic liaisons. Given the opportunity to meet hundreds of men over the course of one or two weeks—many more than one might meet in a normal lifetime—more than one female volunteer succumbed to the charms of young men who played the "I'm going overseas and I might die, so sleep with me tonight" card. It had worked to seduce women in previous wars, and World War II proved no different.

A 1942 conference of the American Social Hygiene Association concluded that promiscuous adolescents (most were under twenty-one and many were under nineteen) practiced "sexual delinquency of a non-commercial character...[seeking] adventure and sociability" and were responsible for much of the spread of venereal diseases. An army doctor who treated VD stated, "While mothers are winning the war in the factories, their daughters are losing it on the streets." In 1943, the Federal Security Agency issued a pamphlet that provided tips on how to prevent the spread of venereal diseases by controlling prostitution and classified amateur "promiscuous" women as a major obstacle to achieving success. Many, the pamphlet continued, were young girls in their teens who practiced "indiscriminate sexual promiscuity" and were, "strictly and realistically speaking," prostitutes.

Of course, seduction was sometimes a two-way street. During the war years, authorities were plagued with the problem of "Allotment Annies," women who married a number of soldiers prior to their shipment overseas and collected the allotments that the military deducted from the GIs' paychecks. These unscrupulous women were not worried about committing bigamy, and they were willing to take the chance that their schemes would never be discovered. All it took to be successful was a few days of sexual activity, a few letters sent overseas and the ability to keep identities straight—it just wouldn't do to call husbands by the wrong names. Some married four, five or six husbands and collected allotments from all of them. The big payoff came when their "husbands" were killed in action and they received the $10,000 insurance check paid to surviving wives.

The moral laxity brought about by fluid social conditions resulted in uncounted sexual liaisons, and these liaisons produced greater difficulties for military and civilian authorities in controlling the spread of venereal diseases. So serious was the threat of venereal disease to the efficiency of the U.S. military that some federal authorities linked its rapid spread to an Axis plot to undermine the fighting efficiency of the American military.

The armed forces produced a series of colorful posters that depicted Hitler, Tojo and Mussolini gloating about the spread of venereal disease among American servicemen.

Realizing that there was little they could do to prohibit male-female contact, the military relied on a multipronged approach to the problem. The military policy followed established procedures, some left over from previous wars, and included education (stressing the importance of continence), case finding, treatment (prophylactic and specific), segregation of infectious individuals, the suppression of prostitution and the provision of wholesome recreational facilities. Trainees were given classes on how to avoid VD, including films that depicted the horrors that such diseases could visit on those who contracted them. Chaplains were utilized to preach the message of avoidance and to stress abstinence, often reminding soldiers to "remember your mothers and sisters." Although usually ineffective as a tool to fight VD, authorities hoped that guilt alone would curb the sexual urges of servicemen, and sometimes they were given a copy of Margaret Scruton's "For Honour and for Her!"

Initially, the War Department adopted a policy of rejecting individuals for service who tested positive for venereal diseases, but by 1942 it had changed the policy to allow induction if the cases were not complicated. Similarly, the military followed a policy, based on a 1926 federal law, of punishing individual servicemen who contracted a venereal disease for "immorality" and reducing them in rank, deducting a portion of their monthly pay, segregating them and restricting them to the barracks or, in extreme cases, discharging them from service with a less-than-honorable discharge. Healthcare professionals deplored the enforcement of this policy since it led to many soldiers concealing infections, trying to treat VD by themselves or using civilian doctors. "Concealment of disease, self-treatment, and treatment by nonmilitary personnel...usually mean[s] inadequate and ineffective treatment, more frequent resistant cases and relapses, unnecessary loss of manpower, and a resultant increase in the spread of the disease," warned one army physician in a report to Congress.

Of particular concern to the United States Army Air Forces was the fact that some flying personnel—pilots, pilot trainees, navigators, gunners, bombardiers—were concealing the fact that they had contracted a venereal disease and, in spite of directions to the contrary, were flying while receiving clandestine treatment involving the extensive use of sulfa drugs. The Army Air Forces had reason to believe that sulfa drugs affected the skills involved

For Honour and for Her!

SOMEWHERE, a woman, thrusting fear away,
   Faces the future bravely for your sake;
Toils on from dawn till dark; from day to day
Fights back her tears, nor heeds the bitter ache;
She loves you, trusts you, breathes in prayer
   your name;
Soil not her faith in you, by sin or shame.

Somewhere a woman—mother, sweetheart,
   wife—
   Waits betwixt hopes and fears for your
   return;
Her kiss, her words, will cheer you in the strife,
   When death itself confronts you, grim and
   stern;
But let her image all your reverence claim,
When base temptations scorch you with their
   flame.

Somewhere a woman watches—filled with
   pride;
   Shrined in her heart, you share a place with
   none,
She toils, she waits, she prays, till side by side
   You stand together when the battle's done.
O keep for her dear sake a stainless name.
Bring back to her a manhood free from shame.

MARGARET SCRUTON

LONDON : THE ALLIANCE OF HONOUR.
Leysian Chambers, 112-114 City Road, E.C.1.

Margaret Scruton's poem "For Honour and for Her!" was handed out to every serviceman during World War II in an attempt to shame the men from having sexual contact with any female other than their wives. *Courtesy of the Camp Blanding Museum.*

in flying, and no one receiving arsenical drugs was permitted to fly. The stigma of being charged with immoral behavior and the possibility of an "undesirable" discharge was enough to persuade these men to try to cure themselves. Army Air Forces physicians recommended that venereal diseases be treated like any other medical problem "in order to save the cost of concealed infections to the Air Forces in men, planes, time, and disruption of training and tactical service, and in order to improve the health, efficiency, and safety of personnel."

Although Congress responded and repealed the law that imposed punitive measures in September 1944, the manpower needs of the services were so pressing that this policy had been largely abandoned as early as 1942.

In recognition that World War II soldiers were no different than their predecessors in other wars, the military also stressed prevention by the use of condoms. "Put it on before you put it in" and "If you can't say no, take a pro[phylactic]" became popular slogans passed along from the War Department to trainees. Posters featuring innocent young girls with the slogan, "She may look clean…but…Pick-Ups, 'Good Time' Girls, Prostitutes Spread Syphilis and Gonorrhea. You can't beat the Axis if you get VD." Still, the onus of the spread of venereal disease was placed on outside sources, and the punishment for contracting one of these was minimal. The explanation that "boys will be boys" exonerated service personnel from any responsibility in the passage of VD to others.

Because of all the training bases in the state, Florida was the epicenter of venereal infections for American troops. As early as the winter of 1941, a spokesman blamed the prostitutes and victory girls in Tampa for the loss of more than fifteen thousand man-days for the United States Army Air Forces alone. On August 26, 1942, the *Tampa Tribune* reported that the city "was the worst spot for prostitution" in the country. In the April 27, 1941 edition of *Time* magazine, Pensacola was labeled "one bad spot in Florida" that was "near the top of the War Department's black list" of worst military towns for VD. Camps Blanding and Gordon Johnston had similar problems, and Blanding in particular had to deal with prostitutes who plied their wares along "Boomtown Road." Jacksonville, Miami, Orlando and smaller towns like Melbourne and Fort Myers faced growing problems with the spread of venereal diseases. As late as January 1944, the *Pensacola Journal* quoted a local VD control officer as placing the number of infected persons in the city's population of 90,000 at "11,000 with syphilis and 5,000 with gonorrhea."

Posters warning servicemen that even the most innocent-looking female was a potential carrier of venereal diseases. "They don't wear labels" was a common slogan used to convey the hidden dangers that lurked in having casual relationships. *Courtesy of the Camp Blanding Museum.*

In a series of articles in June 1942, the *Tampa Tribune* stated that the rate of VD infections among soldiers stationed at local bases had risen from 55 per 1,000 to 88 per 1,000 soldiers tested. For the state as a whole, the VD rate among service personnel tested rose to 170 per 1,000. Certainly, there were many who contracted venereal diseases but were never tested. The civilian population also experienced an exceedingly high growth rate in the number of venereal disease cases. The national average for syphilis hovered around 45 cases per 1,000 men examined. In Florida, however, statistics showed cases in about 157 per 1,000 adult males. Alarmed, the state government tried to remedy the situation. The Tampa Social Protection Division reported an alarming 415 per 1,000 rate of infection for black soldiers.

Because they were more visible to authorities than were the amateur victory girls, military authorities centered their attention on professional prostitutes and called on civilian officials to clean up their cities or face having entire towns declared off limits. With a long history of tolerating vice, Tampa's efforts to clean up local prostitution operations were viewed skeptically by military authorities, who accused the police department of taking bribes and protecting the organizers of prostitution rings. In Pensacola, city fathers agonized over the possibility that unchecked prostitution and the continued growth in the number of persons infected with some form of venereal disease might cause the navy to abandon the city and move its airfields elsewhere after the war. The federal May Act of 1941 gave the secretaries of war and the navy broad powers to deal with prostitution near military installations, including "such steps as they deem necessary" to shut down brothels, bars and other establishments where prostitution flourished. By 1944, the threat of harsh action by federal authorities had led local governments to close red-light districts in their towns. These actions, however, produced undesired results; VD rates continued to climb as prostitutes operated in the shadows.

The reality was that Florida cities were ill prepared to deal with prostitutes. As late as early 1943, the Sunshine State had no laws directly prohibiting prostitution or imposing penalties. Instead, law enforcement officials had to rely on cumbersome vagrancy and loitering laws to arrest both prostitutes and their amateur victory girl competitors. This oversight was corrected when the Florida legislature passed a broad anti-prostitution law in April 1943 that incorporated any sexual act outside marriage as a form of prostitution. The law also gave officials the power to close any establishment—restaurants, hotels, rooming houses or other businesses—that aided or abetted "prostitution, lewdness, or assignation."

In addition, the legislature, citing the court case *Jacobson v. State of Massachusetts*, 197 U.S. 11 (1905), which suspended some individual liberties in the face of public health concerns, created three Rapid Treatment Facilities where those identified with having a venereal disease could be sent—against their will if necessary—for treatment and rehabilitation. Located at former CCC camps in Ocala, Wakulla, Miami and Jacksonville, these centers offered medical treatment, as well as psychological and morality counseling. Medical treatment involved a protracted period and could be as long as five months. The accepted treatment in the early war years was a concoction of arsenic and bismuth. The development and introduction of penicillin in early 1944 made treatment easier in the early stages of syphilis and gonorrhea but did little to cure individuals in advanced stages. Even with the growing use of penicillin as a treatment, VD rates continued to rise.

Cities and counties created Social Protection Divisions, which worked hand in glove with the state board to join with law enforcement officials in order to identify areas of concern and to provide educational materials to better inform the public about venereal disease. In Tampa, the Civil Air Patrol, a group of volunteer pilots, used its planes to drop informative leaflets on city streets. At the insistence of the local Social Protection Divisions, women arrested for prostitution or even for loitering would be given a blood test and an intrusive vaginal examination, usually conducted by male doctors in the jail facility. These women were held for a minimum of four days or until the results of the examination came back. Because authorities cast a large net, many innocent women were caught and arrested. By today's standards, these arrests were often flagrant violations of civil rights, but protests against them were ignored. For example, the *Pensacola Journal* reported the arrest of one sixteen-year-old girl for merely talking with navy aviation cadets in the city bus terminal at 1:45 a.m. Some municipalities tried various systems of identifying non-prostitutes, including the use of "health cards" obtained from local physicians or clinics.

There was a racial aspect to the anti–venereal disease campaign in Florida. Local civilian authorities were quick to place the blame for the spread of the diseases (even in the face of other contributing factors) on the state's indigenous African American population and the influx of blacks from other states. In September 1943, Tampa mayor Robert E. Lee Chancey offered the following comment: "If we had no Negro soldiers here, our record for social protection for military personnel would be one of the finest in the United States." In Miami, the editor of the *Miami Herald* placed the blame for most crime, particularly prostitution, in the city on African Americans. "Negro town has become a den of iniquity," he wrote, "with prostitution flourishing." In rural Brevard County, home to the Melbourne Naval Air Station and the Banana River Naval Air Station, Judge Vassar Carlton made a speech in mid-1942 in which he reported that "five percent of white men in the county and forty percent of 'colored' men were infected with some type of venereal disease." In Tampa, African American soldiers complained bitterly about mandatory venereal disease checks that they were forced to undergo after a visit to the city.

Black soldiers were not the only ones to face additional scrutiny. At MacDill Field, all female visitors to the "Colored Area" of the field were required to have "V-ette" cards, obtained without charge at the Negro USO in Tampa. They were available after the local USO had checked several references and had ascertained that the applicant was in good health.

While statistics did show that African Americans in Florida, men in particular, did have a higher rate of venereal disease, the statistics did not take into account such factors as access to private medical treatment or treatment at facilities outside the state open to white servicemen. Although federal and state governments had established aggressive public health programs to combat venereal diseases, black communities were less likely to receive services or to participate in programs. Poor whites and poor blacks were also more likely to rely on folk medicine treatments (lemon juice for gonorrhea) or superstitions (it was impossible to contract venereal diseases during the full moon) when dealing with venereal diseases. A lack of education also hampered the effectiveness of anti-VD programs by the military, and many African American and white soldiers believed that the use of condoms actually reduced virility. In addition, prophylactic stations were often located in or near police stations, or they were located away from the Negro sections or where they were so far from bus or train stations that the risk of missing transportation back to camp was sufficient to make a soldier go directly to the station rather than out of his way for prophylaxis. It was unfair, however, to blame African Americans for being the major cause of venereal infections around military bases.

Military authorities did not reveal the number of servicemen (and women) who arrived in the Sunshine State already infected. Although sections of towns and cities near bases in the Sunshine State were periodically declared off limits to servicemen, and although military authorities furnished city officials with lists of establishments where personnel reported having contracted VD, the overall effort of the military left a lot to be desired. The responsibility fell squarely on the shoulders of civilian authorities, who did the best they could. In their zeal to protect American servicemen and the economies of their towns, they often resorted to measures that violated the basic civil rights of men and women of all ages and races. To a great extent, the campaigns against VD were successful, and rates of infection declined by 1945. The end of World War II did not end the war on venereal disease, however, and Florida governments continued to battle this plague. As late as 1948, Rapid Treatment Centers in Florida were still in use. When the Wakulla facility burned down, the hospital at the closed Melbourne Naval Air Station was reactivated and used for treatment.

The spread of venereal disease was a legacy that the military left in the Sunshine State. Even now, the war goes on.

Chapter 11

Nazi and Italian POWs

The Axis Foothold in Florida

*I was captured in September 1944 in France, near Epinal. Via Marseille and Oran (Afrika)
and Norfolk, Virginia, I was brought first to Clinton, Mississippi. From there I was brought
to Telogia, where I worked very hard from February to October 1945 in the woods of
Apalachicola. Sitting on top of a pile of timber pieces there happened a truck accident. I was
wounded and immediately brought to the hospital of Camp Gordon Johnston. In the Camp
Gordon Johnston hospital I was very well treated, so that I was able to recover in a fortnight.
I did not go back to the tents of Telogia, but I became an inmate of Camp Gordon
Johnston. There I dwelled in the last house on the camp border, opposite a small building
where on Sundays classical music was being presented.
I first worked in the hospital where I had to inspect every morning all the toilettes in
the hold area, even in the part where colored people were stationed, even the civilians.
With a rubber stick in my hand I was allowed to pass everywhere. After that I had to
clean very long corridor floors. Later I worked in the kitchens and in a store.
I remember the very nice chapel in the camp and a priest whose name was Paul. My best
friend was Rudy Vessely from Vienna. In this camp I remained until the beginning of the
closing about June 1946. Via Camp Shanks and Belgium I was shipped to England.
—Alfred Heimann, German POW, Camp Gordon Johnston*

The United States had been in World War II only a month when the
first German prisoners arrived in the Sunshine State in January 1942.

They were not soldiers or sailors but a motley collection of civilians collected throughout Latin America. Some were ardent Nazis, but sixteen German Jews, male and female, were included in this initial group and received no special treatment. They were taken to Camp Blanding, housed in the former CCC camp on post, held without trial, interned by sex and required to wear fatigues with large white letters—"E.A."—on their backs. "E.A." meant that they were enemy aliens, not prisoners of war, and they were incarcerated for the duration of the war. Blanding was a temporary encampment for them, and they were soon moved to other facilities in Texas, North Carolina and California. For many, the transfer from the bleak and barren cramped stockade (110 by 150 yards) that had been their home at Camp Blanding was traumatic.

Although the first batch of internees passed rapidly through Camp Blanding, they were soon followed by more and more, until the total reached 3,000—about two-thirds of whom were sent to the fifteen sub camps throughout the state. Blanding became a major receiving base camp for prisoners in northern Florida, while on the western side of the state, Camp Gordon Johnston, which operated under the larger Aliceville, Alabama camp or through Fort Rucker, also in Alabama, became a major internee facility. All told, more than 10,000 German POWs were held in guarded camps around the state. Eventually, 435,788 German, Italian and Japanese prisoners would be detained in the United States.

Living conditions varied from camp to camp; some were primitive and remained so, while others were as good as those enjoyed by American military personnel. Some, particularly those associated with American military hospitals in resort hotels, were good enough to cause a few politicians to charge military authorities with coddling prisoners.

The first German military prisoners arrived at Camp Blanding on September 24, 1942, and consisted of men captured from sunken U-boats, as well as some sailors from the German pocket battleship *Graf Spee*, which had been sunk by its crew in the harbor at Montevideo, Uruguay, after suffering major battle damage from a task force of British naval vessels. Within a few months, the number of German naval prisoners numbered 216 men. No longer housed in the former CCC camp, a new site had been constructed about one mile farther away from this site and became one of only four naval prisoner of war camps in the United States.

In November 1943, prisoners from Rommel's famed Afrika Corps began arriving at Camp Blanding and were housed in a separate

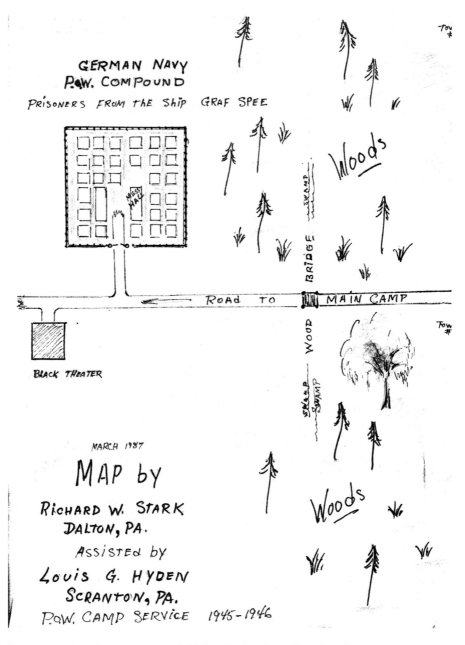

GERMAN NAVY
P.O.W. COMPOUND

PRISONERS FROM THE SHIP GRAF SPEE

Woods

WEST HALL

BRIDGE

SWAMP

ROAD TO MAIN CAMP

WOOD

TOW #

SLASH SWAMP

BLACK THEATER

TOW #

MARCH 1987

MAP by

RICHARD W. STARK
DALTON, PA.

ASSISTED by

LOUIS G. HYDEN
SCRANTON, PA.

P.O.W. CAMP SERVICE 1945-1946

Woods

In 1942, the first German military POWs arrived at Camp Blanding. Survivors of sunken or captured U-boats, the early arrivals were members of the Kriegsmarine, the German navy, and were considered to be elite troops. Even after the arrival of Wehrmacht soldiers, the naval prison compound was maintained separately. *Courtesy of the Camp Blanding Museum.*

Following the success of Allied forces in defeating Field Marshal Erwin Rommel's Afrika Corps, the number of German and Italian POWs exceeded 250,000. With no good place to keep them securely in Europe or North Africa, these POWs were transferred to the United States. Camp Blanding became a distribution base and oversaw their transfer to smaller work camps around the state. *Courtesy of the Camp Blanding Museum.*

compound about a half mile from the naval compound. The decision to separate army and navy prisoners was largely dictated by the U.S. Army's perception of their commitment to Nazism. Naval prisoners, largely from U-boats, were considered to be elite forces, strongly committed to Hitler's ideology. The early prisoners from the Afrika Corps also fell into this category, but by 1943, army prisoner ranks had filled with conscripts, impressed soldiers from areas of Nazi conquest and even some civilian workers captured in various Allied campaigns. Many of the later prisoners were lukewarm or non-supporters of the Nazi ideology, and their lack of commitment to the "cause" created numerous conflicts among the prisoners and headaches for camp administrators. By and large, no such splits existed among naval prisoners of war, and fewer problems arose. Throughout the war, separate compounds were operated for navy and Wehrmacht prisoners of war. Although guarded by American soldiers, the POWs remained under the command of German officers and non-commissioned officers. Officers and enlisted personnel lived in separate billets in camp.

The rapid capture of Sicily and the successful invasion of the Italian mainland again increased the number of German POWs. *Courtesy of the Camp Blanding Museum.*

Table 5
POW CAMPS IN FLORIDA
1942–1948

*Banana River Naval Air Station, Brevard County, FL (branch camp under Blanding, FL)
*Bell Haven, Miami-Dade County, FL (branch camp under Blanding, FL)
*Belle Glade, Palm Beach County, FL (branch camp under Blanding, FL)
*Blanding (Camp Albert H.), Starke, Bradford County, FL (base camp)
*Clewiston, Hendry County, FL (branch camp under Blanding, FL)
*Dade City, Pasco County, FL (branch camp under Blanding, FL)
*Dale Mabry Field, Tallahassee, Leon County, FL (branch camp under Johnston, FL)
*Daytona Beach Naval Air Station, Volusia County, FL (branch camp under Blanding, FL)
*Drew Field, Tampa, Hillsborough County, FL (branch camp under Blanding, FL)
*Eglin Field, Fort Walton Beach, Okaloosa County, FL (branch camp under Gordon, FL)
*Camp Gordon Johnston, Carrabelle, Franklin County, FL (base camp)
*Green Cove Springs, Clay County, FL (branch camp under Blanding, FL)
*Hastings, St. Johns County, FL (branch camp under Blanding, FL)
*Homestead Army Air Base, Miami-Dade County, FL (branch camp under Blanding, FL)
*Jacksonville Naval Air Station, Duval County, FL (branch camp under Blanding, FL)
*Kendall, Miami-Dade County, FL (branch camp under Blanding, FL)
*Leesburg, Lake County, FL (branch camp under Blanding, FL)
*MacDill (Leslie) Field, Hillsborough County, FL (branch camp under Blanding, FL)

*Marianna, Jackson County, FL (branch camp under Johnston, sometimes Blanding, FL, also sometimes Fort Benning, GA)
*Melbourne Naval Air Station, Brevard County, FL (branch camp under Blanding, FL)
*Orlando Army Air Base, Orange County, FL (branch camp under Blanding, FL)
*Page Field, Lee County, FL (branch camp under Blanding, FL)
*Telogia, Liberty County, FL (branch camp under Johnston, FL)
*Venice Field, Sarasota County, FL (branch camp under Blanding, FL)
*Welch Convalescent Hospital, Daytona Beach, Volusia County, FL (branch camp under Blanding, FL)
*Whiting Field, Milton, Santa Rosa County, FL (branch camp under Fort Rucker, AL)
*White Springs, Hamilton County, FL (branch camp under Blanding, FL)
*Winter Haven, Polk County, FL (branch camp under Blanding, FL)

Housing in the compounds consisted of simple, wooden, sixteen- by sixteen-foot "victory-type hutments and mess halls"—canvas tops on wooden frames with six-foot-high wooden walls—similar to those that had been built by the Civilian Conservation Corps in the 1930s and by the first infantry trainees at the base. POWs were required to build their own shelters on the white, soft sand of Camp Blanding. Inside the compound, the native grasses and weeds were removed and the area covered in hard-packed sand. As the camp began to fill up, some areas were sodded. A mess hall, much like the temporary mess hall used by the CCC in its encampments, fed the prisoners.

As the number of POWs increased at Camp Blanding, finding ways to keep them occupied became a problem for the camp's staff. Small gardens and improving the look of the compound occupied the prisoners for a short while, but both POWs and American military authorities worried about keeping them busy and out of trouble. Using scrap lumber and a minimum of tools, POWs soon constructed walkways through the encampment edged with glass soda bottles. Today, these are the only remnants of the POW compound at Blanding. A small canteen and even smaller store were added later and provided prisoners with the opportunity to socialize and to buy small items not provided by the military.

The Wehrmacht compound was surrounded by two fences topped by three strands of barbed wire. Eight guard towers, linked by a catwalk, and floodlights provided armed guards with vantage points to view the camp in its entirety throughout the day and night. Fixed machine gun emplacements were constructed in each of the guard towers. The smaller navy prisoner compound had a similar security system but with only four guard towers and no catwalks. Although the army assigned two military police escort guard companies to guard the POWs, perhaps the greatest security for these compounds were the roughly eighty-thousand-armed American soldiers undergoing training on the post.

The primary concern of the guard detachments was not the possibility of POWs escaping—although several attempts were made—but the prisoner-on-prisoner violence that broke out occasionally between those who had been early arrivals and those who came after them. When the first POWs arrived in late 1942 and early 1943, the outcome of the war was still in doubt. Some of the early arrivals from the German Kriegsmarine, or navy, were extremely patriotic and tried to enforce an unswerving loyalty to Hitler's Germany. Those who spoke out against the war or were perceived as having less than total allegiance to the German cause were beaten or threatened with death. Originally a small group—there were only sixteen POWs in it as of January 1943—the naval compound received an influx of a number of naval prisoners from other camps in the United States, and many of these new arrivals were avowed anti-Nazis. On November 15, 1943, the pro-Nazi elements in the camp staged a strike against the presence of some more moderate POWs in the camp. This was followed a month later by a "riot" that caused the less fervent prisoners to seek safety from the camp guards, who put them into protective custody. Two months later, twenty-four officers in the camp asked for transfers to Camp McCain, Mississippi, a special camp for hardcore Nazis. They did so because Blanding's compound had acquired an anti-Nazi reputation, and they feared for the safety of their families back home in Germany if authorities there thought that they were "guilty by association." Their request was refused, so they voluntarily segregated themselves from the other POWs in the camp. The conflict between pro-Nazi and anti-Nazi prisoners festered in the Blanding navy compound until the end of the war, and authorities tried to deal with the most extreme POWs by transferring them to other camps.

When the first Wehrmacht prisoners arrived in September 1943, Camp Blanding became a major base camp for German POWs. The question of what to do with them was unsettled, although they were put to work maintaining the installations where they were housed. The War Department also authorized the use of POWs for civilian work when the need was certified by the War Manpower Commission. In January 1944, Paul V. McNutt, the chairman of the commission, wrote to Senator Claude Pepper of Florida that he had certified the need for the creation of auxiliary work camps in the state for POWs who would work "in pulpwood cutting and [the] gathering of naval stores." Within a few months, twenty-two branch camps, under the control of authorities at Camp Blanding, had been created, and an additional three branch camps were administered by authorities at Camp Gordon Johnston. Just as quickly, POWs were put to work harvesting citrus, working at a limestone mine manufacturing bricks and on various military bases around the state.

When the first contingent of 250 POWs arrived at Camp Gordon Johnston in March 1944, they were placed in a crudely constructed compound where conditions, like those experienced by American servicemen stationed at the post, were rudimentary. Constructed on sand close to the shores of the Gulf of Mexico, the compound was made up of fifty tents, which housed five to six men, two latrines, a shower tent, a canteen housed in two small tents and a mess hall in a larger tent. The sandy soil was so unstable that construction of recreation facilities, such as a soccer field, was impossible. The only gathering place for the prisoners in their off hours was in the mess hall. Prisoners at Gordon Johnston would endure these conditions until August 1945, when they were transferred to barracks formerly used by American soldiers.

Although originally a branch camp for the larger compound at Aliceville, Camp Gordon Johnston was elevated to the status of base camp after several months. Three branch camps at Telogia, Eglin Army Airfield and Dale Mabry Army Airfield completed the administrative responsibilities for Camp Gordon Johnston. The Telogia camp, located ninety-seven miles west, was a logging camp where workers harvested logs and pulpwood. This was the largest branch camp for Gordon Johnston. POWs at Eglin and Dale Mabry worked in warehouses or performing routine base maintenance.

Telogia, like Camp Blanding, had its problems. In August 1944, POWs working in the logging camp refused to work. What the cause for this work stoppage was is unknown, but after the entire camp population had its rations reduced to bread and water, the POWs went back to work. In October 1944, two POWs at Telogia again refused to work; they were given fourteen days

German POWs were used to perform routine maintenance on airbases and naval bases in the Sunshine State. Most military installations in Florida maintained small groups of POWs, usually 100 to 250, for such work. POWs built the swimming pools at Banana River and Melbourne Naval Air Stations. *Courtesy of the Brevard County Historical Commission.*

incarceration and, once again, were placed on a diet of bread and water. This quick and harsh punishment seemed to bring about the desired effect, and the camp was no longer subjected to work stoppages.

Workers in the branch camps of Camp Blanding and Camp Gordon Johnston performed a variety of jobs and generally enjoyed better conditions than those who remained in the base camps. Perhaps the 264 POWs at the Kendall base camp had it best of all. The men were housed in four barracks "well arranged in palm and pine woods" with a view of the gardens. Kendall's POWs were used as gardeners, hospital workers, mechanics, electricians, painters and kitchen helpers in the large Miami Beach hotels that the War Department had requisitioned for American soldiers recuperating from wounds or other illnesses. The Kendall camp became the focus of a congressional investigation led by Congressman Robert Sikes, who charged that the POWs were being coddled. Although the U.S. Army experienced little trouble with the prisoners in the Kendall camp, two of them, Willi Severitt and Rolf Schenkel, did try to escape. The men surrendered five days later, after going two days without food.

The branch camp at Drew Army Airfield in Tampa was another compound that had better-than-average accommodations for POWs. Authorities converted four large barracks, formerly used by the base's WAC detachment, for use by the POWs. Although conditions at the camp were good, the prevalence of a large number of unrepentant Nazis kept the POWs in an uproar by holding "celebrations with National Socialist content." Robert D. Billinger Jr., author of *Hitler's Soldiers in the Sunshine State: German POWs in Florida*, quoted one former prisoner who worked at Drew Field and saw this firsthand: "The overwhelming spirit was…Nazi in the camp." Work slowdowns, a lack of military courtesy on the part of POWs and a general lack of discipline were noted by Major Edward C. Shannahan, a field liaison officer, and he put much of the blame on the poor supervision of the guards overseeing the prisoners.

Much the same could be said about the supervision of guards at other camps. The Orlando Army Airfield was home to 636 POWs—later 756—who were housed in four separate companies in rather comfortable barracks. Although the POWs were supposed to be used to supplement civilian labor, the base's provost marshal and intelligence officer feared escapes to such a degree that most of the POWs remained on the post doing basic maintenance work. Major Shannahan, on an inspection tour of the facility, noted that the few POWs who actually performed work in the civilian sector had been misused. After a meeting with the provost and intelligence officer, changes were made. Soon, more than 600 of the prisoners were busy working in citrus groves, packinghouses, plant nurseries and canneries.

In Dade City in Pasco County, POWs worked in citrus groves and packinghouses. In Belle Glade, prisoners were put to work on truck farms or in bean canneries. Clewiston, perhaps the worst of the branch camps, employed POWs cutting sugarcane eight hours a day. Leesburg, in Lake County, was another branch camp that employed prisoners in citrus groves, packinghouses and canneries. The branch camp at Winter Haven also used POWs to pick and process citrus. Prisoners at the branch camp in White Springs were put to work cutting pulpwood and digging firebreaks through the forest. At Eglin Army Airfield, Banana River NAS, Melbourne NAS, Whiting Field, Page Army Airfield, Venice Army Airfield, Jacksonville NAS and other, smaller USAAF installations in the Sunshine State, POWs were

Camp Gordon Johnston also had a population of POWs, who worked on maintenance at the base. Some worked in the base laundry or, like these prisoners, in the camp bakery under the direction of an American serviceman. *Courtesy of the Camp Gordon Johnston Association Museum.*

put to work on base maintenance projects. In Daytona Beach, some 250 POWs were assigned to work in Welch General Hospital and remained there until late 1946.

In an interesting aside, American inspectors who visited the agricultural work camps noted how fascinated the German POWs were with reptiles, including rattlesnakes and alligators. Several remarked that POWs, working in the forests or sugarcane fields, captured rattlesnakes and alligators. The alligators they intended to keep as pets, but the rattlesnakes were killed and their skins cured to make wallets and belts. It was, one supposes, a learning experience.

The use of POWs as workers in civilian enterprises was profitable for the U.S. Army. Private contractors were charged the prevailing hourly or daily rate, but POWs were paid only eighty cents a day, which was placed in their accounts at the camp canteen. The remainder of the wages paid was turned over to the federal government and used to underwrite the expenses of maintaining the camps. On March 9, 1945, Captain Leon Theil, the public relations officer for Camp Blanding, published an article in the *Bradford County Telegraph*, in which he placed the amount of money generated by POW labor at $777,058.81 in the last four months of 1944. The POWs were paying their own way and, more importantly, were easing the manpower shortages that existed in Florida. Hopefully, he added, the generous American treatment of German POWs would result in similar policies by the Germans toward American POWs in the *stalags*.

Despite the large numbers of German POWs scattered around the Sunshine State, there was only a small number of attempted escapes. Billinger categorizes three types of would-be escapees—the individualists, the threatened and the alienated. Of the thirty-three escapes from Florida camps, five were the work of two men: Fritz Dreschler, who fled three times—twice from the Orlando Army Airfield camp and once from Camp Blanding—and Bruno Balzer, who managed to escape twice from Camp Blanding.

A third prisoner, Karl Behrens, escaped from the Clewiston branch camp and was found hanging from a tree two days later. Apparently depressed at receiving no mail from home and alienated from his fellow companions, Behrens fled the camp and committed suicide. Eliot Kleinberg, in his 1999 book, *War in Paradise: Stories of World War II in Florida*, gives a detailed account of Behrens's life and experiences as a POW. He was the only POW escapee to avoid recapture.

Fritz Dreschler, the so-called "escape king" of German POWs, was certainly an individualist. A member of the Sixteenth SS Division, he was captured in Italy in 1944 and soon arrived in Florida. Assigned to the Orlando Army Airfield, he first escaped in January 1945, the same day that Karl Behrens was found hanging just a couple of miles from the Clewiston branch camp. For thirteen days, Dreschler evaded authorities, who were searching frantically for him. Newspapers were filled with sightings of the escapee and with news of two other escapees, Harry Fischer and Gunther Gabriel, who had managed to slip away from the Dade City branch camp on January 5. By January 7, all three prisoners were back in the hands of military authorities and back in camp. Gabriel and Fischer were found in a sealed boxcar in Jacksonville, which they had hoped would take them to New York and a chance to escape via a ship leaving that port. Dreschler was returned to the Orlando camp.

The reports of escaped prisoners that appeared in the Tampa and Orlando newspapers were unusual because the military and the Federal Bureau of

Investigation, which had overall responsibility for tracking and recapturing escapees, actively pursued a policy of downplaying escapes. Because local law enforcement agencies and the general public were essential to spotting escapees, this "hush-hush" policy was not very effective, and newspapers vied with one another to generate the most sensational headlines. When Fritz Dreschler escaped the second time and was recaptured, the July 13, 1945 edition of the *Tampa Morning Tribune* used the headline "Nazi Caught Here Wearing Two Pink Panties," while the *Palm Beach Post*'s headline was a more moderate "Nazi POW Escapee Captured at Tampa." Dreschler had apparently been caught with the underwear, along with other items of clothing, that he had purloined from a private residence.

Dreschler's third escape came in January 1946 from the Camp Blanding base camp, where he was awaiting repatriation to Europe. Rumors in the camp insisted that the POWs would be repatriated first to France to help rebuild that country and then to the region where they had joined the German military. As a member of the SS and a veteran of fighting on the eastern front, Dreschler had no desire to go to France or to face the revenge of the Russians, who now occupied his hometown.

Bruno Balzer, a two-time escapee from the naval POW compound at Camp Blanding, was one of the alienated POWs. His opinion that Germany was losing the war did not sit well with the majority of POWs in the compound, and he took to his heels after he was threatened. His initial escape was in February 1945, and he was quickly captured. Four months later, in June, Balzer joined four other prisoners in a bid for freedom. Four of the five were taken into custody almost immediately, but Balzer managed to hide out for four days before he was captured.

Johann Klapper, a POW in the camp at MacDill Army Airfield, disappeared from the compound in March 1946. For three months, he managed to elude American authorities by hiding in a hole underneath a building on the base. Managing to survive on food he scavenged from nearby mess halls and drinking water that trickled through the floor of the building from a leaky refrigerator, he was finally caught on June 19.

Other POWs managed to escape for short periods. Franz Drews fled the branch camp at Winter Haven in July 1944 but was recaptured four days later. In May 1944, Walter Weber and Joseph Summerer escaped from the compound at Dade City, but their bid for freedom was short-lived. So, too, was the escape of Gunther Gabriel and Harry Fischer in January 1945 from the same camp. The final escapee from the Dade City branch camp was Hermann Hanns, who managed to elude recapture for eighteen days. Gerhard Anklam and Wilhelm Stuttgen, two POWs working in the sugarcane fields around Clewiston, managed to escape the camp and remain free for three days. They were captured just thirty-five miles from the camp.

Walter Jentsch, another SS soldier, escaped from the POW branch camp at the Daytona Beach NAS in September 1945, long after the war in Europe was over. Like Fritz Dreschler, Jentsch might have been apprehensive about the reception he would receive in postwar Europe. He managed to make it to Miami Beach before he was recaptured a week later.

By late 1945, Camp Gordon Johnston had closed, and responsibility for German POWs was transferred to Fort Benning, Georgia. By mid-1946, Camp Blanding no longer housed a POW population, and the remaining prisoners were transferred to Jacksonville NAS. Full repatriation would not be completed until 1948.

Table 6

POW ESCAPES FROM FLORIDA CAMPS

Billinger, *Hitler's Soldiers in the Sunshine State*

MONTH/YEAR	CAMP	LAST NAME
May 1944	Dade City	Summerer/Weber
July 1944	Camp Blanding	Klassen/Kunkel
	Winter Haven	Drews
August 1944	Telogia	Bach/Kruetner
		Schulze/Weilgohs
September 1944	Kendall	Schenkel/Severitt
	Gordon Johnston	2 unnamed
January 1945	Clewiston	Anklam/Stuttgen
	Clewiston	Behrens
	Clewiston	Pernull
	Dade City	Fischer/Gabriel
	Orlando	Dreschler
February 1945	Blanding	Balzer/Rogalla

Month/Year	Camp	Last Name
	Dade City	Hanns
March 1945	MacDill	Klapper
June 1945	Blanding	Balzer/Hilkenmeir
		Fitzner/Schmitt
		Nachenhorst
July 1945	Orlando	Dreschler
September 1945	Daytona Beach	Jentsch
October 1945	Blanding	Skof
January 1946	Blanding	Dreschler

Across the United States, some 2,222 German POWs tried to escape. Florida's 33 escape attempts by POWs were the lowest in the nation. Perhaps the rural nature of Florida, the vast distances that had to be traveled and the absence of large ethnic German populations in the Sunshine State contributed to the lack of success for escapees and prevented more POWs from trying. Perhaps the warm weather, good food and generally pleasant conditions in the branch camps also contributed to the acceptance of their fate by the prisoners. The warm relations of local Floridians that the POWs found when they worked in civilian industries might also have dampened their desire to escape. Many of the POWs who were assigned to branch work camps carried pleasant memories of their time in the Sunshine State, and some bring their families over to revisit the people they met and the places they worked as POWs. In places like Dade City and Telogia, local residents still remember the POW camps and harbor warm feelings toward the Germans who occupied them.

Chapter 12

WAR ON TWO FRONTS

Soldiers of Color in Florida

Fourteen millions of loyal Americans have the right to expect that in a war for the advancement of the "Four Freedoms" their sons be given the same right as any other American to train, to serve, and to fight in combat units in defense of the United States in this greatest war in its history.
—*U.S. Representative Hamilton Fish (R-New York), 1943*

Look here, America
What you have done—
Let things drift
Until the riots come
Yet you say we're fighting
For democracy.
Then why don't democracy
Include me?
I ask you this question
Cause I want to know
How long I got to fight
BOTH HITLER—AND JIM CROW
—*Langston Hughes, "Bequmont to Detroit," 1943*

Although African American soldiers had distinguished themselves in all previous wars fought by Americans, especially the Civil War and World War I, the idea of black soldiers, airmen and sailors as frontline personnel was an anathema to military leaders. In 1940, African Americans could not serve in the Marine Corps or Army Air Corps, they were assigned only menial positions in the navy and they were inducted into the army in limited numbers and placed in segregated noncombat units. Despite the fact that the Selective Service Act of 1940 prohibited discrimination because of race and color, the armed forces, usually citing low educational scores and poor overall general health, were slow to accept African American draftees. There was some truth to this concern since the army used the Army General Classification Test (AGCT), which had been designed to measure an inductee's ability to learn and to be trained for military duties. The median score expected for those taking the test was 100; white draftees had an average score of 107, while the average for black draftees was only 79. The test scores reflected the substandard education that most African Americans received in the years before World War II, particularly in the South. Additionally, local draft boards, especially those in the South, were overwhelmingly made up of white citizens, whose racist perceptions of blacks were that they were cowardly, disloyal and intellectually and morally unfit.

The United States Army Air Forces was the most adamant in refusing to accept black inductees, arguing that flying and maintaining aircraft demanded technical skills beyond the ability of most blacks to attain. USAAF planners explained that the best use of time and money was to accept only those trainees who had the potential to master the difficult tasks that operating an air force required. Any time taken to educate and train poorly educated African Americans was simply not the most efficient use of defense budgets or the best use of the limited number of instructors. In addition, the USAAF, following the general policy of the American military to maintain segregated units—of which the USAAF had none—rejected applicants since its leaders did not consider the USAAF the proper agency to correct social problems, especially during wartime. The navy did accept African American volunteers but assigned them to maintenance or galley duties. The majority of blacks were assigned to shore duty, including security and labor details and working as yeomen, storekeepers and in other capacities. Likewise, the army accepted volunteers and draftees but only in segregated units in support roles. Throughout the services, segregation was the governing policy.

Although the navy accepted African American enlistees, it initially assigned them to mess duties. Toward the middle of World War II, black sailors were also placed in support units but were not allowed to become pilots or ships' officers. *Courtesy of the Brevard County Historical Commission.*

Under pressure from black leaders, President Franklin Roosevelt instructed the War and Navy Departments to begin accepting more blacks. On June 1, 1942, the U.S. Marines organized a "Negro Battalion" for the first time in its history. Howard P. Perry became the first African American to enlist in the U.S. Marines and broke a 167-year-old barrier. The first class of twelve hundred black volunteers began its training three months later as part of the Fifty-first Composite Defense Battalion at Camp Lejeune, North Carolina.

In 1941, the War Department forced the newly formed Army Air Forces to accept blacks for the first time. Once the gates were opened, thousands of African Americans joined the USAAF. While a few did become pilots—most notably the Tuskegee Airmen—most blacks in the air forces were assigned to Engineer Aviation Battalions (EABs). Of the 157 EABs that saw duty in World War II, forty-eight were all-black units.

EABs were created to construct airfields in newly liberated territories in Europe and the Pacific. While all members of EABs received spotty training at best, black units were given even less training. Frequently assigned to menial chores in addition to their training duties, training was often interrupted or postponed so that these chores could be done. For example, black soldiers from the 857th EAB, in training at Eglin Field in north Florida, were so busy doing menial labor on the post that they participated in only one field training problem, the completion of a heavy bar and rod runway. On the other hand, the 810th EAB, another all-black unit, received six months of training with heavy equipment and built roads and bridges at MacDill Field before it went overseas.

African American political leaders protested the discrimination against inducting blacks into the military. On September 17, 1940, prominent black leaders met with the secretary of the navy and the assistant secretary of war to demand the mobilization of more African Americans, including the induction of black nurses, more black men in flight training schools and the total desegregation of the armed forces. Although federal officials made promises, little in the way of concrete actions was taken. In December 1941, the month the United States entered the war, there were only 13,200 African Americans in the army and a mere 4,000 in the navy. The official policies of the United States military were also firmly established this month: segregated units and no combat training. The Japanese attack on Pearl Harbor readily exposed the fallacies of these policies when Doris "Dorie" Miller, a navy mess attendant on the USS *West Virginia*, manned a .50-caliber machine gun and subsequently downed two attacking planes, despite never having fired the weapon before. Although Miller was awarded the Navy Cross for his heroism, he remained a mess attendant until his death aboard the USS *Liscome* on November 24, 1943.

Some black leaders did not sit idly by without protesting the blatantly discriminatory policies of the United States military. In January 1942, Ernest Calloway, a labor activist and a member of the group Conscientious Objectors Against Jim Crow, refused induction because of the segregationist practices of the military. Calloway and other blacks who refused to serve were incarcerated, but their protests did not produce changes in the way the armed services treated African Americans.

Military authorities placed a quota on the number of black inductees who were to be accepted into the armed forces. Since African Americans constituted about 10 percent of the total population of the United States,

In the army, African Americans were slowly accepted. Those who were drafted or enlisted were usually relegated to support units commanded by white officers. The army did allow for black officer candidates to attend the same training schools as white candidates. This is a photograph of the all-black 337th Service Band stationed at Camp Gordon Johnston. *Courtesy of the Camp Gordon Johnston Association Museum.*

this was to be the maximum number of inductees. As late as 1943, however, Paul V. McNutt, the chairman of the War Manpower Commission, complained to the head of the Selective Service Commission, General Lewis B. Hershey, that African Americans made up less than "six percent of our armed forces." As late as September 1944, the 701,678 black troops in the army composed only 8.7 percent of the total number of soldiers. In the navy, the percentage was even less. Only the Coast Guard, which integrated its personnel early on, could boast of adhering to both the spirit and the letter of the nondiscriminatory provisions of the draft law.

With the passage of the Selection Service Act of 1939, the military was hard-pressed to find places to train the inductees, and new camps were constructed in great haste. Because of the large spaces needed for training and the need for facilities that would allow for year-round training, most of these new bases were built in the rural South or Southwest. When the bases were completed, segregated barrack areas for African American troops and separate recreational and service facilities were the norm. As late as May 1944, Charles F. Wilson, a soldier stationed at an army airfield in Tucson, Arizona, complained in a letter to President Roosevelt about conditions at the base:

This African American naval company was based at Melbourne NAS and was utilized as waiters and cooks in the officers' mess. *Courtesy of the Brevard County Historical Commission.*

Negro soldiers are completely segregated from the white soldiers on the base. And to make doubly sure that no mistake is made about this, the barracks and other housing facilities (supply room, mess hall, etc.) of the Negro Section C are covered with black tar paper, while all other barracks and housing facilities on the base are painted white.

At Camp Blanding, black troops in Detachment A, the support unit for the post, were housed in a separate area between white troops and the POW camp and forced to use separate recreational facilities. White troops and German POWs swam in Kingsley Lake, while African American soldiers were required to use Lake Whitamore, a smaller lake with a less desirable beach.

The prevailing system of Jim Crow that dominated the South exacerbated the problems faced by African Americans soldiers. Many, if not most, of the officers commanding black troops were white, and many were southerners.

Although the army integrated its officer training schools early on as a cost-saving measure, black officers were seldom given command responsibilities but were assigned as junior officers in support units. Even the basic military courtesies were often denied them. In June 1944, Reverend Adam Clayton Powell Jr., a New York civil rights leader, received a letter from an anonymous soldier from California that detailed the experience of one black officer:

> *On August 31ˢᵗ 1943, a white private told a Negro Officer who had reprimanded him for not observing the ordinary military courtesy of a salute, if you would take your clothes off and lay them on the ground I would salute them but I wouldn't salute anything that looks like you. The Officer called a Captain and told him of the incident. In the presence of the private, the Captain said, "Well, Lieutenant, what do you want me to do about it?"*

The same letter cited the experiences of four

> *Negro Officers…[who] when they arrived on the post they found signs on the latrines of the post "COLORED TROOPS NOT ALLOWED." These officers photographed these signs the following day. That afternoon, the Commanding Officer of the post removed the signs. Later that evening, he called in these Officers and told them that the post was a "Keg of Dynamite" and he wanted us to tell our boys to overlook the little insults and incidents, and not start any disturbance. They couldn't win anyway, and after all only northern Negroes are insulted by the use of the term Nigger. A Southern boy understands that the white man means no harm when he uses that term. It is needless to say that the Negroes told him that they would not carry any such message to the boys and it is needless to say that they didn't.*

Such incidents were not unusual. In Florida, black troops also experienced the same kind of discrimination and harassment on posts. In his article, "G.I. Joe Meets Jim Crow: Racial Violence and Reform in World War II Florida," Gary Mormino cites an instance that occurred in November 1942 in Tallahassee: "A black soldier at Dale Mabry Field violated racial decorum when he attempted to purchase a drink from a vending machine reserved for white civilians. Scores of black soldiers and whites scuffled, resulting in injuries to eight individuals." This was only one of what would be several confrontations between black servicemen and whites in Florida's capital.

Watts Sanderson's "jook" in Tampa was a favorite meeting place for off-duty African American soldiers in the Tampa area. *Courtesy of the Robertson-Fresh Collection, University of South Florida Special Collections.*

In Jacksonville during the summer of 1942, an altercation between two black soldiers from Camp Blanding led city police to beat several African Americans at the scene and to quarantine the city's black community. For several days, law enforcement officers patrolled the area armed with shotguns and submachine guns. In a September 1943 report, the FBI quoted an informant who blamed any racial conflict in the city on the influx of "many strange faces among the Negroes." The informant went on to state that the local "problem among the Negroes is becoming more acute daily since so many Negroes are in the Armed Forces that expect and assert their demands for the same privileges as are enjoyed by the white men in the Armed Forces." A second informant corroborated this opinion by placing the blame for any "unrest, dissatisfaction and trouble among the Negroes" on the "influx of many northern Negro civilians and soldiers."

War on Two Fronts

The report described an event that took place on June 24, 1943, when

> *a company consisting of Negro soldiers at Camp Blanding, Florida staged a dance at the camp. Members of another Negro company, Company D, milled about the dance and staged something similar to a demonstration. When ordered away by Military Police, they became angered and resentful. Subsequently, members of Company D gained access to gun racks that had been left unlocked and secured fourteen rifles, as well as ammunition that had been left over from range practice and war games. They fired rounds of ammunition into the crowd at the dance, and as a result nine Negro girls, eight Negro soldiers and one white officer received wounds.*

Lieutenant Gabriel Lazar was a white officer at Camp Blanding who encountered the pernicious racism that black soldiers had to deal with. He was assigned to escort two busloads of African American troops from Tallahassee to Camp Blanding. Although they carried their lunches, they had nothing to drink with them. Lazar stopped the convoy at a roadside diner to purchase soft drinks for the troops and to allow them to use a restroom. The white proprietor of the diner refused to allow the black soldiers access to the restroom or to sell them sodas. Lazar then purchased ninety soft drinks for his men, but the two white bus drivers refused to help him carry them to the buses. He did it by himself.

In May 1943, the report continued, black soldiers attached to an engineering battalion working on the construction of the Cross City Army Airfield

> *attempted to associate with white residents, especially in bars and eating places theretofore restricted to white people. A number of these soldiers were northern Negroes...It is further reported that on one occasion Negro soldiers chased a proprietor out of his place of business after he had allegedly advised them, "niggers" were not permitted to come into his place of business.*

The FBI concluded its report on the Cross City incident with the warning that "the white citizens of the city allegedly began arming themselves in preparation for additional advances by Negro soldiers." An unknown soldier stationed at the Cross City base commented on conditions in the town:

> *As you have perhaps gathered by now, we are in Cross City, God help us. We can rightfully call ourselves the A.E.F.—Americans exiled in*

Florida...One thing we have an abundance of here, mosquitoes and every species of insects imaginable giant sizes. Mosquitoes grow three and four times as large as they do at home...Clouds are gathering for a storm, but it sure is hot. Am sitting outside on a little entrance porch to the barracks and the sweat is pouring off me. Oh, for a little New England weather... About the only redeeming feature of the town is that liquor, are only fifteen cents a drink, thirty cents a double shot. The boys sure have done their part in consuming the liquor...Have perhaps mentioned in a previous letter that the town is rather rough, and that there have been a number of knifings and killings and at least every Saturday night, everybody come to town then there is some sort of a brawl...Fortunately last night I did not go to town. There was a little excitement. A colored soldier knifed a civilian. Immediately afterward, the M.P.'s were in town and all the boys had to come back to camp at 10:15 P.M.

In Pensacola in 1943, a near riot erupted when two white policemen arrested a black soldier for striking a white man. In the course of making the arrest, one of the policemen struck one of the African American servicemen who had gathered at the scene. Only the timely arrival of reinforcements—more city policemen and military police from Pensacola NAS—prevented a large-scale outbreak of more violence. Not all the opposition to blacks in military service came from the local community. In 1944, Robert Sikes, longtime Panhandle politician and a member of Congress, complained to the navy that he had received reports of black and white sailors at the Pensacola NAS sharing the same billets. Rear Admiral George D. Murray hastily reassured him that "in no cases is the indiscriminate mixing of these groups permitted."

Tampa, which was branded one of the eleven centers of repression in the United States by the American Civil Liberties Union, and Tallahassee were the centers of conflict between black servicemen and the local whites. In June 1943, a conflict occurred between a white saleswoman in the post exchange and a black soldier, and a fight began. Some black soldiers returned to their barracks and armed themselves with weapons. Nineteen African American soldiers were arrested and charged with participating in a conspiracy to riot and mutiny. Ten of the arrested soldiers were subsequently court-martialed and sentence to long prison terms. In February 1944, a police narcotics raid in the city's black district escalated into a full-fledged riot when a black serviceman cursed a white army captain, T.L. Tedford, and military police arrested him. An estimated crowd of four thousand blacks demanded the soldier's release, and police called for reinforcements. Over one hundred military and civilian policemen, armed with machine guns and revolvers, managed to disperse the mob.

In 1944 and 1945, African American soldiers were involved in public brawls and riots in Tallahassee during a series of minor altercations between soldiers from Camp Gordon Johnston, sixty miles south of the city, and those stationed at nearby Dale Mabry. Some confrontations were caused by black versus black incidents, while others pitted white soldiers against black ones. In some instances, black soldiers rebelled against the unfair treatments they received under the South's prevailing Jim Crow system. African American women also served in the military and also experienced segregation. The forty black women who entered the first WAAC officer candidate class at Fort Des Moines, Iowa, were placed in a separate platoon. Although they

The African American USO Club in Tampa is an example of how a segregated military was more costly than an integrated one because on-post and off-post facilities had to be duplicated. *Courtesy of the Florida State Photographic Archives.*

The USO Club for African Americans in Daytona Beach was rather small and nondescript. This group of soldiers, probably from Camp Blanding, seems to be enjoying its visit. *Courtesy of the Florida State Photographic Archives.*

attended classes and mess with the other officer candidates, post facilities such as service clubs, theatres and beauty shops were segregated. Black female officer candidates had backgrounds similar to those of white female officer candidates, and almost 80 percent had attended college and had work experience as teachers and office workers.

Although equality in the American military would not come for several years after the war, the refusal of blacks to placidly accept less-than-equal treatment during World War II would bear fruit when, in 1948, President Harry S Truman ordered the desegregation of all branches of service.

Segregation in the American armed forces in World War II and the services' policy of not allowing blacks to fight in combat roles until near the end of the war was an expensive proposition. Not only was it necessary to build separate facilities on military posts, but also much of the administrative expenses were inflated. Although the cost in dollars was much more than would have been spent on an integrated military, the real cost came about

When compared to the African American USO in Daytona Beach, the USO for white soldiers in Sebring seems absolutely plush. Certainly, there appeared to be significant differences in the quality of opportunities offered to black and white troops. *Courtesy of the Sebring Historical Society.*

because of the loss of critically needed manpower for Allied offensives. Even civilian organizations like the USO and Red Cross found it necessary to operate separate facilities on posts and in towns. Every major town near a military base had two USOs—one for white soldiers and one for blacks.

White soldiers sometimes attended events at black USOs, but the favor was not returned. In Fort Myers, McCollum Hall was built by Clifford McCollum in 1938 in the Dunbar community, and during the war, its second story was redesigned to house a large dance hall and a raised stage for live performances. The second floor also served as the USO for African American troops stationed at Page and Buckingham Fields, and "big bands" regularly performed there. It was common to find white residents and soldiers in attendance at these performances.

Whatever the cause, African American soldiers in Florida and other parts of the South were the victims of on-base and off-base violence from whites.

All in all, 2.5 million African American males registered for the draft, and 1,056,841 served in some capacity. Members of the African American press and black political leaders continued to point out the similarities between the racist policies of the Axis powers and the discrimination suffered by black service men and women. The black press urged African Americans to embrace the "Double V" campaign—victory against the Axis and victory at home—over racial discrimination.

Service in the armed forces brought revolutionary changes to the African American community that would eventually result in a successful drive for civil rights and first-class citizenship in the 1960s. A majority of the black men who served came from the plantations and small towns of the South. Just as it had in World War I, service outside of the South and outside of the country gave many African Americans a lasting taste of fair treatment and social freedom, an experience they shared with many black workers who went north to work in defense industries. The association of southern African Americans with blacks from the North, who usually had higher expectations of equality and repudiated Jim Crow more vocally and insistently, increased their sense of self-worth and self-respect. Although racism was a day-to-day reality in the armed forces of the United States, participation in military service provided training, education and new skills. In one survey, 41 percent of black servicemen, compared to 25 percent of whites, expected to be better off because of their service and cited future gains in acquiring more of the rights and privileges exercised by white Americans. As a result of their experiences, African Americans, particularly those from the South, gained a new sense of geographic mobility, which expressed itself in the movement of black veterans to different sections of the nation after the war.

Chapter 13

OF SMALLER UNITS AND SPECIAL TRAINING

The development of the amphibian tractor, or LVT, which began in the middle 1930s, provided the solution and was one of the most important modern technical contributions to ships-to-shore operations. Without these landing vehicles our amphibious offensive in the Pacific would have been impossible.
—Lieutenant General Holland M. Smith, USMC

Although there were many large military bases in the Sunshine State during World War II, there were also a number of small bases, some used for training and some performing top-secret work. One of the most unusual of these bases was a small, unobtrusive facility located at Jupiter Inlet, known as "Station J," which monitored the low-frequency transmissions of German U-boats prowling off the coast of Florida. Using a variety of intercept equipment to determine the positions of the U-boats, the information was relayed to American or other Allied ships, which would then hunt and destroy the enemy vessels. More than sixty-five U-boats were sunk off the coast of Florida, largely due to information provided by the monitoring station.

From 1940 until 1945, the small post grew from a small complement of thirty-five service personnel to ninety-five, including marines stationed there as guards. As the war wound down, so, too, did the importance of this station. By July 1945, the monitoring station was turned over to the Coast Guard and all monitoring activities ceased.

Donald Roebling, the grandson of the designer and builder of the Brooklyn Bridge, was a wealthy resident of Clearwater. His father, John A. Roebling, witnessed the devastating loss of life caused by the hurricanes of 1926, 1928 and 1932 in the Everglades and southern Florida and challenged his son to invent a vehicle that would go just about anywhere on land or water. In 1933, Donald Roebling set about designing such a vehicle. In early 1935, he introduced the Alligator, a large, boatlike vehicle made of aluminum, propelled by rubber treads and powered by a small engine. The invention caused a sensation, and *Life* magazine featured it in an October 4, 1937 article.

Rear Admiral Edward C. Kalbfus, the commander of the American battleship fleet in the Pacific, saw the article and shared it with Major General Louis McCarty Little, the commanding general of the fleet marine force, who then forwarded it to the commandant of the Marine Corps with a recommendation that the corps explore the possible use of Roebling's invention as a landing boat. Although the investigating officer, Major John Kaluf, recommended that the corps purchase a test vehicle in 1938, the Marine Corps Equipment Board turned down his recommendation because of budgetary constraints. Following a change in the board's personnel, another visit to the Roebling factory in Dunedin was scheduled, and the new board chairman, Brigadier General Emile P. Moses, persuaded Roebling to design a stronger and more powerful version that would meet the needs of the marines. Although there was no funding for the new project, Roebling took the $18,000 needed from his own pocket, and design and testing of the improved version of the Alligator went forward.

Although the Alligator 2, completed in May 1940, was a more robust vehicle, it still did not meet the requirements of the Marine Corps. Later that year, the Navy Bureau of Ships awarded a $20,000 contract to Roebling to build an even more powerful Alligator 3. Completed in October 1940, the new vehicle met most of the marine's requirements when it was tested at Quantico, Virginia, and in the Caribbean. With a few more modifications, the new Alligator was accepted by the navy, and Roebling received a contract, the first of what would be several contracts, for one hundred of the vehicles. Roebling set about producing hundreds of Alligators in factories at Lakeland, Florida, and Riverside, California, owned by the Food Machinery Corporation of Dunedin. In February 1941, the navy ordered an additional

The Roebling Alligator, invented to provide safe travel in the Everglades after hurricanes, was quickly adapted for military use in World War II amphibious landings. The United States Marine Corps trained with Alligators in Dunedin. *Courtesy of the University of South Florida Special Collections.*

two hundred Alligators, now called LVTs, and began to organize specialized units to operate them.

Improvements to the LVT continued throughout the war, including the addition of armor and a tank turret. The Alligator proved its worth at the battle for the island of Guadalcanal, where it was used to support marines fighting in thick jungle terrain. Eventually, every marine division included an amphibious assault battalion equipped with Roebling's Alligator. Even today, the U.S. Marines continues to use variations of Roebling's original design to carry out amphibious landings and to offer close armored support for infantry units.

The Marine Corps quickly established a presence in the Dunedin area. In February 1941, Major George W. McHenry, USMC, was assigned to the FMC plant in Dunedin to oversee the production of the first batch of Alligators. On May 2, 1941, a U.S. Marine Corps Amphibian Tractor Detachment was activated at Dunedin under the command of Major William W. Davies. Major Davies, along with four marine officers and thirty-three enlisted marines,

Navy officials watch the loading of a Roebling Alligator onto a ship. The Alligator was modified, up-armored and equipped with machine guns. One version featured a turret gun from a Sherman tank. *Courtesy of the University of South Florida Special Collections.*

tested new LVTs and established the first amphibian tractor school. Using the Hotel Dunedin as its base until barracks and maintenance facilities could be built, this first amphibian tractor detachment worked out the intricacies involved in using the Alligator in landings. By September 1941, a steady flow of marines was headed for Dunedin, where, upon completion of the training provided by Major Davies and his instructors, they were assigned to the newly activated First Amphibian Tractor Battalion. By mid-February 1942, the First Amphibian Tractor Battalion was complete with companies (each company was equipped with one hundred LVTs), plus a headquarters and service company, and was assigned to the First Marine Division. Six months later, in August 1942, the First Amphibian Tractor Battalion was part of the amphibious assault on the Japanese stronghold on Guadalcanal. By this time, the Second Amphibian Tractor Battalion had been established at Camp Pendleton, California.

In addition to the U.S. Army's amphibious training base at Camp Gordon Johnston and the Dunedin training base, the navy also set up a base at Fort

The navy created a "Scouts and Raiders" school in Fort Pierce, which also included a training program for amphibious watercraft drivers. Eventually, Fort Pierce became the center for training Underwater Demolition Teams (UDTs), which evolved into modern-day SEALS. *Courtesy of the SEAL Museum, Fort Pierce.*

Pierce in late 1942. This base was a little different, however, and concentrated on teaching scouts and raiders the finer points of blowing up beach obstacles. When amphibious training was discontinued at Camp Gordon Johnston, much of the equipment and many of the army instructors were transferred to Fort Pierce to become part of the navy's program. The army and navy jointly established the Amphibious Scout and Raider School. Lieutenant Commander Phil H. Bucklew, the "Father of Naval Special Warfare," helped organize and train the navy's "first group" to specialize in amphibious raids and tactics. This "Scouts and Raiders" unit was first employed in Operation Torch, the invasion of North Africa in November 1942.

In June 1943, the navy decided to create and train a large dedicated force of men for amphibious forces and to start experimental work and training for permanent naval demolition units for assignment to various combat theatres. On May 7, Admiral Ernest J. King, the chief of naval operations, picked Lieutenant Draper L. Kauffman, a demolitions expert, to lead the

UDTs were trained to deal with obstacles, including natural ones, which impeded amphibious landings. Operating in small teams, the UDTs were the original "frogmen" of the U.S. Navy. *Courtesy of the SEAL Museum, Fort Pierce.*

Higgins boats, which ferried troops to landing beaches, were commonly used in UDT training at Fort Pierce. This boat had a specially modified bow that provided additional strength to the landing ramp as soldiers disembarked. *Courtesy of the SEAL Museum, Fort Pierce.*

training, which was to be based at Fort Pierce, Florida. Fort Pierce was selected because of the number of beaches and estuaries that could be used to mimic conditions along European and Pacific beaches and because the mild water temperatures allowed for year-round swimming training.

The initial group of trainees, volunteers from the Seabees, marines and army combat engineers, arrived in June 1943 and immediately underwent a grueling week of intensive physical training designed to "separate the men from the boys." This was the first of the famous "Hell Weeks" that would become the hallmark of Underwater Demolition Team (UDT) training (and later SEAL training in the modern navy). As soon as the conditioning phase of the training was completed, the UDTs were given extensive training in disarming, arming and using explosives that might be encountered on enemy beach obstacles or used to destroy them. The UDT training staff was tasked with a two-part mission: (1) the demolition of man-made obstructions and the destruction or removal of mines on approaches to beaches, and (2) the improvement of beach approaches to allow for the expeditious landing of troops and supplies.

Residents in nearby Fort Pierce soon became used to hearing explosions going off night and day as the UDTs practiced raids. Farther south near Jupiter Inlet, residents of Stuart and Jensen Beach could count on hearing explosions as well. Even today, residents of the area find practice bombs and unexploded ordnance on the beaches and the shoreline of the Indian River Lagoon. Despite the noise and the inconvenience of leftover explosives, residents of south Florida fondly remember the men who trained as Underwater Demolition Teams.

"It seems there's a place in Florida," remembered one UDT graduate, "between the towns of Jensen and Stuart, which is just nasty enough for demolition to [be] practiced there." Another UDT member recalled:

UDTs used long tubes of explosives to destroy obstacles that prevented amphibious landings. Although this scene is of trainees at Fort Pierce, the obstacles they encountered were typical of real obstacles that were in place on enemy beaches. *Courtesy of the SEAL Museum, Fort Pierce.*

Of Smaller Units and Special Training

Although they were members of the navy, trainees at Fort Pierce utilized army fatigues, equipment and weapons. Many of the instructors who had been part of the army's amphibious training program at Camp Gordon Johnston were transferred to the base at Fort Pierce, making the school there a combined effort of both branches of the American military. *Courtesy of the SEAL Museum, Fort Pierce.*

We worked on blowing a deeper channel from the ocean to the Indian River. We called the place JenStuFu. The cold, miserable conditions, along with sand fleas, cold water and C&K rations trained us to be able to take most any kind of conditions and respond adequately.

Once the ten-week course at Fort Pierce was through, graduates were shipped off to California and the Hawaiian island of Maui for additional training if they were slated to go to the Pacific. Those assigned to the European theatre in preparation for the Normandy invasion completed their final training in the British Isles.

The army and navy, along with the Coast Guard, opened training facilities for women in the service. The Coast Guard provided training for SPARS, as

Above: WAVES played important roles in the operations of naval bases in Florida. In this photograph, a member of the WAVES, who is also a member of the base staff, stands at Saturday morning inspection at NAS Melbourne. *Courtesy of the Brevard County Historical Commission.*

Left: Ruth Rubin Elsasser, a Miami resident, became one of the first officers in the WAVES. Along with her three brothers, all of the Rubin siblings served in the military. Her brother Jack was held as a POW in Germany. Because the Rubin family was Jewish, they worried about how Jack would be treated by the Nazis. *Courtesy of the Irving Rubin Collection, the Florida Historical Society.*

female members were called, at Henry Flagler's old Ponce de Leon Hotel in St. Augustine, while the navy (WAVES) and army (WAACs/WACs) operated training bases in Daytona Beach. More than twenty thousand WAVES graduated from the Daytona Beach NAS facility. Soon, every major military installation in the Sunshine State boasted a complement of female service personnel performing jobs ranging from clerical work to operating control towers and training classes.

When navy/Coast Guard recruiters visited the Tampa Bay area in 1943, more than 150 women applied for service in the WAVES or SPARS, a feat that was matched just a few months later when army recruiters came to town seeking women for the WACs. African American women were recruited for the services, and many joined, although they experienced the same kinds of discrimination as male recruits did.

Two women's groups—the Women's Flying Training Detachment (WFTD) and the Women's Auxiliary Ferrying Squadron (WAFS)—were combined in July and August 1943 to create the Women Airforce Service Pilots (WASPs), comprising privately trained pilots who ferried all types of American aircraft around the globe, tested new aircraft at factories and often towed targets for bomber gunners to shoot. Under the command of Jacqueline Cochran, a native Floridian, the skilled pilots of the WASPs flew every type of aircraft produced for the United States. Although they were not members of the armed forces, the WASPs were very much in evidence at airfields in Florida. Morrison Army Airfield in West Palm Beach was the major transit point for airplanes going to both the European and Pacific theatres of operation, and hundreds of female pilots passed through. They were regulars on routes that included flying over the Atlantic Ocean to Africa and then to Australia or Burma.

On December 20, 1944, the WASPs were officially disbanded. At the last graduation program for WASPs, General Henry H. "Hap" Arnold commended them:

> *You and more than 900 of your sisters have shown that you can fly wingtip to wingtip with your bothers. If ever there was any doubt in anyone's mind that women can become skillful pilots, the WASP[s] have dispelled that doubt. I want to stress how valuable I believe the whole WASP program has been for the country…We know that you can handle our latest fighters, our heaviest bombers; we know that you are capable of ferrying, target towing, flying training, test flying, and the countless other activities which*

*you have proved you can do. So, on this last graduation day, I salute you
and all WASP[s]. We of the Army Air Force are proud of you; we will
never forget our debt to you.*

In 1977, President Jimmy Carter signed the GI Bill Improvement Act, which granted WASP pilots full military status. In March 2010, surviving members of the WASPs were awarded congressional Gold Medals.

At Cross City Army Airfield and at Orlando Army Airfield, units of the army's Chemical Warfare Branch conducted tests of chemical defoliants on Florida forests. A favorite testing site was the Withlachoochee Land Reclamation area outside Brooksville because the heavy growth of some of the more remote parts of the project approximated the jungle growth of combat areas in the Pacific theatre of operations. This secret project tested early variants of Agent Orange, the defoliant used during the Vietnam War, before they were shipped overseas for use in combat areas.

At Key West, the navy conducted its "Sub-Chaser School," which trained almost fifty-eight thousand men and women from the United States and Allied countries in methods of applying modern technology in U-boat searches. Key West, which saw its population grow from a prewar four thousand to forty-five thousand by 1945, was also home to a major installation for lighter-than-air aircraft—blimps—that patrolled the shipping lanes along the coast of the Sunshine State. Although blimps were able to spend a long period aloft and enjoyed expansive views of the ocean, they were also subject to hostile fire from U-boats and lacked the ability to maneuver quickly. On July 18, 1942, a patrolling blimp was shot down by the guns of a German submarine. All hands were rescued by a destroyer, but the incident served to remind Floridians that war, indeed, had come to the Sunshine State.

In the major colleges and universities in the Sunshine State, the armed forces utilized existing facilities and expert faculty members to teach numerous programs, ranging from accounting to math. The University of Miami was a favorite of the navy, while the army made use of the University of Florida at Gainesville and Florida State College for Women (now Florida State University) in Tallahassee. Many of the individuals who attended these universities under the auspices of the services would return later to take advantage of the GI Bill.

One of the most interesting units in Florida during World War II was the Civil Air Patrol (CAP), which was part of the Florida Defense Force, a temporary replacement for the National Guard, which had been

WACs lead a parade in downtown Jacksonville in 1944. The growth of the number of women in the military forces of the United States after 1943 demonstrated the same principle that industrial leaders were learning—women were competent and eager workers whatever role they were assigned *Courtesy of the Florida State Photographic Archives.*

federalized. The CAP was a collection of private pilots who used their own aircraft to fly antisubmarine patrols along Florida's beaches. Although it was in existence for only a short time—from 1941 until 1943—the Civil Air Patrol made a significant contribution to the war effort, including several important missions undertaken for civilian authorities. The CAP was based at established military bases on the coasts of the Atlantic Ocean and the Gulf of Mexico.

Not all of the World War II military installations in Florida were large, but they all were important to the ultimate success of the Allied cause.

Chapter 14

WAR PROPAGANDA

American Style

Under their system, the individual is a cog in a military machine, a cipher in an economic despotism; the individual is a slave. These facts are documented in the degradation and suffering of the conquered countries, whose fate is shared equally by the willing satellites and the misguided appeasers of the Axis.
—Government information manual for the Motion Picture industry, Office of War Information

Although Americans liked to rail against the broadcasts, speeches and writings of Nazi propaganda minister Joseph Goebbels, the government of the United States and private enterprise made heavy use of propaganda in a variety of ways. By attributing animalistic, demonic and otherwise undesirable characteristics to their appearance, American propagandists attempted to demonize wartime enemies and to galvanize the public against them. The vicious atrocities committed by Axis armies in Europe and the Pacific provided enough reality-based ammunition to make even the most nonsensical parodies seem truthful. Japanese, Italian and German leaders were portrayed as evil or comedic figures, either subhuman or superhuman, but never normal humans.

In every sector of American society, every branch of the military, every government agency and every war industry trained graphic artists and

This is the Enemy

WINNER R. HOE & CO., INC. AWARD – NATIONAL WAR POSTER COMPETITION
HELD UNDER AUSPICES OF ARTISTS FOR VICTORY, INC - COUNCIL FOR DEMOCRACY - MUSEUM OF MODERN ART

Caricatures were often used to depict the German military as haughty and unfeeling Prussians, a holdover from the propaganda used in World War I. Dehumanizing and demonizing the Germans and Japanese were commonplace tactics in American propaganda posters and advertising. *Courtesy of the Camp Blanding Museum.*

maintained printing operations to produce leaflets, pamphlets and posters to pound home the message that the war was a contest between good (Allied) and evil (Axis). The principal method used by Americans to convey this message was the printing of posters. In fact, more propaganda posters were produced in the United States than in any other country, Axis or Allied, during the war.

Although American propagandists denigrated the work of Goebbels, they often imitated his techniques. After Leni Riefenstahl's *Triumph of the Will*—a film about the Nazi convocation in Nuremberg in 1934—premiered in 1935, the success of this film both commercially and artistically, to say nothing of its emotional and intellectual appeal to Germans, established a pattern that American filmmakers would later follow. Frank Capra, a noted

"Der Fuehrer's Face," a song from the Disney cartoon of the same name, was popular during World War II. The Southern Music Publishing Company used these cartoon characters on the cover of its sheet music to the song. *Courtesy of the Camp Blanding Museum.*

Hollywood producer, began producing a series of seven films, collectively entitled *Why We Fight!*, in 1942 and finished the series in 1945. Using copied German and Japanese film and combat footage, Capra merged them into films that damned the Axis powers in their own words. Walter Huston, an Oscar-winning actor, narrated the films, and the script he read made use of racist and nationalist rhetoric. President Franklin Delano Roosevelt, who saw the first film in the series, was so moved by it that he urged its showing in "every public arena."

The Walt Disney Studios and other cartoon producers in Hollywood produced animated films with the same themes, although they lacked the realism of *Why We Fight!* In some ways, the use of popular cartoon characters—Mickey Mouse, Donald Duck, Fitz the Kat and a host of other characters—was even more effective than the movies with actors. The short length of cartoons—three to four minutes—held the attention of audiences, and the cartoon violence against stereotypical Axis figures met with loud applause. The Disney cartoon, *Der Fuehrer's Face* or *Donald Duck in Nutziland*, produced a popular hit for bandleader Spike Jones and his orchestra:

> *Ven der Fuehrer says, "Ve iss der master race,"*
> *Ve HEIL!* [honk!] *HEIL!* [honk!] *Right in der Fuehrer's face!*
> *Not to luff der Fuehrer iss a great disgrace,*
> *So Ve HEIL!* [honk!] *HEIL!* [honk!] *Right in der Fuehrer's face!*
> *Ven Herr Goebbels says, "Ve own der world und space,"*
> *Ve HEIL!* [honk!] *HEIL!* [honk!] *Right in Herr Goebbels' face!*
> *Ven Herr Goering says, "Dey'll never bomb dis place,"*
> *Ve HEIL!* [honk!] *HEIL!* [honk!] *Right in Herr Goering's face!*

The Walt Disney Studios and other cartoon artists lent their skills to designing everything from nose art for bombers to individual unit patches and signs for bond rallies. Even envelope and stationery manufacturers added bestselling lines that featured cartoons of Axis leaders printed on the front. Not all propaganda art was aimed at "tickling the funny bone"; some deliberately played on the heartstrings of the public by incorporating pictures of soldiers in combat or enemy forces engaged in atrocities. Dire warnings—"Loose Lips Sink Ships" or "The Enemy is Listening"—on posters and signs alerted citizens that failure to heed the warnings could possibly lead to disaster. Advertisers quickly adopted support for war activities as major themes in ads. Buying the product advertised, the unstated message implied, would somehow help win

Right: Cartoonist Dick Oyer designed this logo for antisubmarine units of the navy stationed at Mayport Naval Station near Jacksonville. His style was typical of the hundreds of professional and amateur artists who produced cartoon art for military units. *Courtesy of the Beaches Historical Society, Jacksonville Beach.*

Below: This preprinted envelope was typical of the kinds of stationery bought by servicemen and sent home to anxious families. The comedic portrayal of Hitler was intended to allay any worries that families might have had about the safety of their sons. *Courtesy of the Camp Blanding Museum.*

World War II propaganda art often featured scenes of combat that were designed to instill a sense of fear as a way of motivating Americans. This painting for an Orlando bank's war bond drive warns that, unless patrons buy bonds, an attack on their town might happen. "Bonds Stop Bombs" was the simple message on how such an attack might be prevented. *Courtesy of the Orange County Regional History Center.*

The makers of Chesterfield cigarettes were only one of thousands of manufacturers to incorporate war themes into their advertising. Notice the pictures of service personnel on the individual cartons. *Courtesy of the Camp Blanding Museum.*

the war. Mass advertising performed a dual purpose—not only did it sell products to the public, but it also conveyed a jingoistic sense of nationalism to that same public. No product was too small to advertise, nor was any chance missed to drive home this dual purpose. From gasoline to soap, many companies used this kind of advertising to entice consumers to buy their product, but they promoted patriotism at the same time.

Even respected news media outlets abandoned their claims to impartiality and made use of images that conveyed the idea that German and Japanese leaders and soldiers were subhuman. On the cover of its December 7, 1942 issue that marked the anniversary of the Pearl Harbor attack, *Time* magazine feature a portrait of Admiral Ernest J. King looking steely-eyed into the distance, while caricatures of the swastika and rising sun (with the scowling

Admiral Ernest J. King, the chief of naval operations, was featured on the cover of *Time* magazine on December 7, 1942. *Courtesy of the Camp Blanding Museum.*

visage of a Japanese man) faced the guns of an American battleship. Two months later, *Time* featured a cover with a picture of Japanese admiral Osami Nagano gleefully looking at the reader, while behind him a cartoon battleship with a menacing, grinning face and a pointed pistol conveys a sense of violence. The message was unmistakable: Allied leaders were high-minded, reluctant warriors, and Axis leaders were violent, untrustworthy gunslingers who would kill anyone.

One of the most interesting uses of propaganda was in popular radio programs of the war years. While American heroes like the Shadow and Superman—often using verbiage that reinforced the idea that the men and women they fought were animals—faced and triumphed over villainous German and Japanese spies, many of the programs ended with a public

Japanese admiral Osami Nagano, the chief planner for the Imperial Navy and King's counterpart, was caricatured on the cover of *Time* in February 1943. *Courtesy of the Camp Blanding Museum.*

service message that encouraged Americans to practice racial tolerance, perhaps a tacit recognition of the reality of the Jim Crow system in the United States.

Floridians and their fellow American citizens flocked to the movies, and movies, too, contributed to the propaganda effort. Virtually every movie produced during the period from 1942 to 1945 touched on the war effort in some way. *Casablanca* (1942), *Wake Island* (1942), *Corregidor* (1943), *Bataan* (1943) and *Flying Tigers* (1942) were just a few of the movies produced during the war, but the movie propaganda effort against the Axis powers had started earlier. Charlie Chaplin starred in *The Great Dictator* (1940), a satirical look at Adolph Hitler, and *A Yank in the RAF* (1941), which depicted the heroic efforts of American volunteers in the Battle of Britain. By 1945, movies, such as *They Were Expendable* (1945), about the war in the Pacific theatre were being filmed in the Sunshine

This 1942 poster by J. Howard Miller was originally made for the Westinghouse Corporation but gained widespread popularity as a Rosie the Riveter poster. The model for the poster was Geraldine Doyle, a Michigan factory worker. *Courtesy of the Florida Historical Society.*

State. More than static posters and pamphlets, movies brought the war to life, and patrons could vicariously experience the thrills, danger and excitement of fighting the war while absorbing patriotic fervor. Movies were also used to ease the transition of GIs back into American society. William Wyler's *The Best Years of Our Lives* (1946) graphically portrayed the difficulties encountered by returning servicemen in adapting to civilian life.

Most propaganda was aimed exclusively at Americans in an effort to get them involved in the war effort. Women, in particular, were targets for propaganda campaigns that encouraged them to enter the labor force to fill the vacancies left by men who had entered the armed forces. Beautiful, though muscular, depictions of women, complete with rolled-up sleeves and bandanas, were commonplace, and most carried the simple message, "We Can Do It!"

Noted graphic artist Norman Rockwell introduced Americans to his version of Rosie the Riveter with this May 29, 1943 cover of the *Saturday Evening Post*. Mary Doyle (now Mary Keefe), a nineteen-year-old telephone operator in Arlington, Vermont, was the model for Rockwell's painting. *Courtesy of the Camp Blanding Museum.*

Propaganda art could be fine art with enduring value. On the cover of the May 29, 1943 issue of the *Saturday Evening Post*, artist Norman Rockwell created the ultimate propaganda image of workingwomen when he painted an idealized portrait of Mary Doyle (now Mary Keefe), a nineteen-year-old telephone operator in Arlington, Vermont. The original painting by Rockwell now resides in the Crystal Bridges Museum in Bentonville, Arkansas. The museum acquired it for an unspecified price, but the last public auction of the painting at Sotheby's in 2002 brought a sale price of $4.96 million.

World War II propaganda was not solely the work of professionals. Schoolchildren around the nation were often encouraged to create posters that incorporated patriotic themes. Awards and small cash prizes were frequently given in recognition of the art produced by students, and some manufacturers sponsored national campaigns to encourage them to produce more.

Although Americans often publically ridicule propaganda efforts, the reality during World War II was that they readily identified with the messages that were put before them in every imaginable medium. The fact that they were already preconditioned to accept the messages made absorbing them easier.

Chapter 15

VICTORY AT LAST!

Florida Returns to Normalcy

The Allied Armies, through sacrifice and devotion and with God's help, have wrung from Germany a final and unconditional surrender.
—President Harry S Truman, May 1945

The Governments of the United States of America, the Union of Soviet Socialist Republics, the United Kingdom and the Provisional Government of the French Republic, hereby assume supreme authority with respect to Germany, including all the powers possessed by the German Government, the High Command and any state, municipal, or local government or authority. The assumption, for the purposes stated above, of the said authority and powers does not effect the annexation of Germany.
—U.S. Department of State, 1945

It is my earnest hope—indeed the hope of all mankind—that from the blood and carnage of the past, a world founded upon faith and understanding, a world dedicated to the dignity of man and the fulfillment of his most cherished wish for freedom, tolerance, and justice [will emerge].
—General Douglas MacArthur, aboard the USS Missouri, August 14, 1945

Although the German offensive, commonly called the Battle of the Bulge, in December 1944 came as a complete surprise to American military leaders, the final defeat of Germany was a foregone conclusion. On the eastern front, Russian troops pushed beleaguered German forces closer and closer to Berlin, while British and American bombers continued their around-the-clock raids in the face of an almost nonexistent German air force. In the Pacific, Japanese forces were retreating toward their home islands as the combined air force, navy and army forces of the United States hopped from solitary outpost to solitary outpost, repealing the advances that the Empire of Japan had made in the early years of the 1940s. They, too, faced final defeat, although the willingness of Japanese forces to surrender made a final date for the end of the war problematic. Total victory against the Axis was certain, and only a few months remained. German forces surrendered unconditionally on May 7, 1945, to end the war in Europe. Japanese surrender would not come until August 14, and then only after the United States had dropped atomic bombs on Hiroshima and Nagasaki.

Floridians, joined by naval personnel, celebrate the news of Germany's surrender on May 7, 1945. V-E Day was the name given to this important day, although the Allies realized that Japan, the remaining Axis power, was still fighting. *Courtesy of the Beaches Historical Society, Jacksonville Beach.*

Victory at Last!

Miami residents spontaneously celebrate the end of the war in the Pacific in a massive crowd that paraded down East Flagler Street. V-J Day—victory over Japan—meant that all of the fighting was now over. *Courtesy of the Florida State Photographic Archives.*

In the United States, war industries, which had produced the materiel that accounted for much of the Allied victories, were gearing down. As the Allied victory became more and more apparent, manufacturers assembled teams of experts to begin planning for postwar activities. Some of the larger and long-established industries, like the Detroit automobile companies, planned to resume prewar manufacturing programs, producing automobiles for civilian markets. Indeed, manufacturers of consumer items of all kinds developed plans to immediately resume their prewar activities as soon as the war ended, hoping to reap great profits from buyers who had been unable to buy such goods during the war.

In the Sunshine State, postwar changes happened at a rapid pace. The economic boom created by the entry of the United States into World War II ended suddenly for Tampa residents, and sixteen thousand shipyard workers faced a loss of work and the end of their jobs. By August 12, despite the absence of a formal surrender by Japan, both the navy and the Maritime Commission had cut back their orders for ships. Two days later, TASCO announced a reduction of its labor force by two thousand workers. On August 17, McCloskey's Hooker's Point yard announced the loss of its contracts. In rapid succession, the *Tampa Tribune* announced one layoff after another. The phaseout was hardly a gradual process; layoffs were frequently for thousands of workers at a time. Although TASCO officials tried to replace shipbuilding with manufacturing travel trailers, they met with little success. George B. Howell, the dominant force behind TASCO, resigned the presidency of the company and returned to the banking business.

By December 1945, the Hooker's Point yard and Tampa Marine had closed permanently, taking with them the large payrolls that had fueled the local economy. Maritime Homes, the large complex erected for war workers at Hooker's Point, was bulldozed. The City of Tampa, which had counted on the $105 million in wages and salaries paid to TASCO workers during the war, now found itself scrambling for tax monies to pay for the improvements it had made to its infrastructure during the war and for providing basic social services to the thousands of laid-off workers, most of whom remained in the city in hopes of finding new jobs.

Tampa residents celebrate the Allied victory over Japan on August 14, 1945. With Japan's surrender, World War II was finally and officially over. *Courtesy of the Anthony Pizzo Collection, University of South Florida Special Collections.*

Victory at Last!

Residents of Tampa's Ybor City celebrate the end of the war from their balcony on Seventh Avenue overlooking the tumultuous activities of the crowd below. *Courtesy of the Anthony Pizzo Collection, University of South Florida Special Collections.*

Young residents of Ybor City lead a parade down a city street following the surrender of the Japanese on August 14, 1945. Note the Cuban flag carried proudly side by side with the American one. *Courtesy of the Anthony Pizzo Collection, University of South Florida Special Collections.*

Matt McCloskey, the developer of Hooker's Point, now shifted his attention once again to traditional construction enterprises, although he did purchase an interest in a Jacksonville shipbuilding company. He surfaced again in the national spotlight in later years as a major developer of Philadelphia real estate and a major contributor to the Democratic Party.

For the residents of Tampa, the end of the war did not mean an end to the industrial dreams spurred by the war. For the next twenty years, various attempts would be made to keep Tampa shipyards in operation. The irony is that the Japanese, whose defeat was engineered, in part, by Tampa workers, would later prove to be too strong as competitors for this industry. So remarkable was the Japanese economic recovery from the war that it would be regarded as nothing short of a miracle. Throughout the 1960s and 1970s, Japanese competition with American industries would see the demise of many segments of the American economy and a corresponding

Newspapers issued special edition after special edition as information flowed into newsrooms following the Japanese surrender. This group of sailors looks at the third "extra" of the *Miami Herald* with satisfaction that the mission had been accomplished. *Courtesy of the Florida State Photographic Archives.*

rise in Japanese industries. "Japan might have lost the war," remarked one politician in the early 1970s, "but it is winning the peace!"

What was true in Tampa was also true in Jacksonville and Panama City, where shipyard workers were abruptly terminated when contracts were rescinded. The large Wainwright Shipyard in Bay County, created almost overnight to meet the demands for new ships in 1941, simply closed its gates with little fanfare. The St. John's River Shipbuilding Company and Gibbs Shipyard in Jacksonville followed suit; so, too, did the Pensacola Shipyard and Engineering Company in Bayou Chico and the American Machinery Company's boatyard in DeLand. The thousands of workers who had been recruited from across the South suddenly found themselves unemployed and at loose ends. Officials in Bay, Duval and Hillsborough Counties struggled to find replacement industries for those they had lost to the war's end.

Not all industries that felt the icy hand of canceled government contracts were big. Across the Sunshine State, small, specialized manufacturing companies faced the immediate postwar years with little hope of continuing production. Adding to the problem of closing factories, thousands of returning veterans, demobilized and unemployed, returned home and immediately began to look for work. Women who had joined the labor force in large numbers and had provided much-needed labor during the war were not asked to go back to their homes and leave the reduced number of jobs open to veterans. Some did leave the workforce willingly, but others clung adamantly to the jobs they occupied.

Unlike World War I, however, the demobilization of American armed forces was not sudden, nor was it total. The occupations of Japan and Germany demanded the continued use of a force larger than the prewar military, and while many veterans were released from service, the draft continued to take men from the labor force. In addition, civilians were also employed in a number of reconstruction jobs, utilizing American labor and that of former enemy soldiers. Reconstruction also continued to fuel some American industries for the next several years.

By 1944, it was evident to most Floridians that the tide of the war had turned in favor of the allies and that the conflict would soon be over in Europe and the Pacific. Former four-time congressman Millard Fillmore Caldwell, a Tallahassee lawyer, was elected governor in November 1944, and in his address to the legislature in April 1945, he emphasized postwar development and economic issues, indicating that Floridians needed to look forward to the end of the war and to plan for Florida's role in the postwar era.

The tourist economy in the Sunshine State was the earliest to reestablish itself during the mid-war and postwar period. Although the military had requisitioned hundreds of luxury hotels for barracks, schools and hospitals, by 1943 hotel operators and state tourism officials had begun campaigning to woo tourists to Florida. As the war wound down, many of the hotels occupied by the military were retuned to their owners, although some of them were much worse for wear and had to be immediately remodeled or renovated. Soon, however, Florida was averaging more tourists visiting the state each year than it had ever had before. The more than one million men and women who were stationed or trained in Florida harbored fond memories of their time here, and they were among the first visitors in the postwar seasons. By the 1960s, tourism became the major industry of the Sunshine State.

Many service men and women also returned to the state as permanent residents and contributed to the dramatic increase in its population, which numbered almost 3 million residents in 1950. With the exception of 2008 and 2009, the population of Florida continued to grow until its current 18.5 million residents made it the fourth most populated state in the nation. Certainly, this was a decided change from 1940, when the Sunshine State was the least populated state in the South—twenty-seventh in the nation, trailing Georgia, Mississippi and Alabama.

During World War II, Florida produced record amounts of mullet and mackerel for the war effort, with over fifty million pounds netted and added to the nation's food supply. Along the Gulf and Atlantic coasts, hundreds of companies geared up to meet the increasing demand for Florida seafood, a demand that continued to grow after the war. Many of these wartime operations still thrive today, although recent bans on net fishing and on the catching of certain species have had a negative impact.

Agriculture was one of the three major elements of the Florida economy in the postwar period. In 1942–43, Florida became the top citrus-producing state in the country for the first time, surpassing California. In 1942, Florida citrus growers patented a process to make frozen concentrated orange juice, and by 1946, millions of gallons flowed from the state's processing plants into the world markets. The state's cotton industry, which had been in the doldrums since the early 1930s, expanded as it slowly became more mechanized, a necessity to compensate for the exodus of cheap labor, mostly African Americans, from the state. In 1945, researchers in Orlando discovered an insecticide, DDT, which became available for commercial use and changed Florida's agricultural industry. DDT proved an effective weapon against a wide variety of insects, including Florida's nettlesome mosquitoes, although this "miracle weapon" would prove to have long-lasting and devastating consequences on native wildlife. In the mid-1940s, however, DDT was highly praised and used widely.

Florida's cattle industry also prospered during the war years and afterward. The cattle tick, long a bane to beef production, was brought under control by insecticides and arsenic dipping. Although the use of these measures would eventually prove to be harmful to the environment of the state, cattle producers were enthusiastic supporters of such programs and immediately began to improve the quality of their stock by importing purebred cattle or by crossbreeding native Florida stock with purebred Brahman, Hereford, Black Angus, Santa Gertrudis and other heavier, meatier breeds.

As returning GIs married and started families, they fueled a building boom in the Sunshine State. No longer willing to live in multigenerational families, they made use of the GI Bill, officially titled the Servicemen's Readjustment Act of 1944, which included a program for low-interest, zero–down payment home loans. With the end of the war, building supplies became increasingly available. Across the United States, suburbs, once considered the domains of the wealthy and upper classes, sprang up. William Levitt pioneered the creation of "Levitttowns," which took the techniques of mass production and assembly lines and applied them to home building. Thousands of small suburban communities sprang up, featuring street after street of identical houses. Tampa entrepreneur Jim Walter, who founded Jim Walter Homes in November 1946, used $395 in savings to build his first "shell" home, a simple structure that featured a completed roof, outside walls, floors and interior stud walls. Situated on a homeowner's lot, buyers could purchase a basic home for one-third the cost of a traditional home and finish the interior of the house as time and money permitted.

A building boom swept through the Sunshine State, rivaling that of the 1920s. An article in the January 1948 issue of *American Builder* noted, "It is expected that the public will be home-conscious for many years, their appetites whetted by several years of shortage." That was certainly true in Florida as residents flooded the marketplace, competing with seasonal visitors—"snowbirds"—for housing. Wilbur Kroetz, a Fort Lauderdale builder, offered "mansionettes" on Miami Beach for $4,995, small studio apartments that included a kitchen, bath, "living-bedroom" and tiled terrace.

Prices for these small dwellings immediately began to escalate and continued to do so throughout the remainder of the 1940s.

Not all changes occurred in cities. In 1940, the Rural Electrification Administration (REA), a New Deal agency operating under the Department of Agriculture, brought electrical power to farms. During the immediate postwar years, this effort continued, and by 1950, more than 1.7 million of the nation's farms had electricity for the first time.

The GI Bill was created to prevent a repetition of the Bonus March of 1932 and to head off a relapse into the Great Depression. One of its provisions was the 52:20 rule, which provided veterans with a weekly stipend of twenty dollars while they were looking for work, guaranteed for a full year. Designed to take the pressure of finding jobs off the former service men and women, this provision did just that. Overall, however, the nation's economy was booming, and less than 20 percent of the funds set aside for unemployment compensation was spent. The GI Bill also provided loans to veterans to create small businesses, and the Sunshine State experienced a boom as new businesses opened to cater to the increasing consumer demands of a growing population.

For ambitious ex-GIs, the bill provided generous payments for vocational training and higher education. Florida's public colleges, which had suffered from neglect during the 1930s, found themselves faced with more applicants than they could accommodate. Many ex-servicemen, whose education had been disrupted by military service, sought to return to school to complete their degrees, and they were joined by thousands of others, many of whom could never have afforded college before, demanding new programs. In 1945, Florida had two state universities, which were for whites only and not co-ed, and a black college, FAMU, which was all-black and co-ed. Responding quickly to the need for an expanded system of higher education, the Florida legislature made both white universities coeducational and increased spending for all higher education units. A system of community colleges was established for major population centers, and although they operated with poorly defined missions, these small institutions relieved some of the pressure on the larger schools. The community college system, a legacy of World War II, continues to function today and serves as "feeder" institutions for the state's eleven universities.

The tremendous growth in population that marked the postwar years in the Sunshine State also produced a number of problems. As early as the mid-1940s, Florida officials articulated concerns over what the rapid growth was doing to the environment. Governor Millard F. Caldwell, who was elected in

1944, convened a special commission to study the problem of limited water supplies and the possible contamination of the state's aquifer by residential development and business expansion. In 1947, the legislature appropriated $2 million to purchase private lands to add to the Everglades National Park in an attempt to keep this fragile ecological area safe from developers.

By 1948, the state began experiencing financial problems brought about by the continuing population growth. As the state's universities and colleges admitted more students, the demand for new buildings for classrooms and dormitories, plus additional buildings for sports and cultural programs, made state spending imperative. The growth of residential communities mandated larger expenditures on roads, bridges and other infrastructures that needed to be built. The war years had been good years for the state's treasury, but within three years, budgetary shortfalls demanded radical action. The state's constitution had been amended in the 1920s to prohibit any imposition of income taxes, so the legislature, called into special session to deal with the financial crisis, approved a 3 percent sales tax, which momentarily solved the problem. Continued growth, however, meant new budget crises in the decades that followed. More and more, state, county and local officials looked to tourism to solve their monetary problems.

Rapid change came to the military in Florida, as well. Large bases, which had fed thousands of trained personnel into all branches of the service, faced closure or reductions in force. Camp Gordon Johnston, which had encompassed 155,000 acres of panhandle land, was closed in late 1945. All base buildings, with the exception of a few housing units built for officers, were bulldozed and burned. The acres of land that had once made up the camp were returned to their original owners or sold to new ones. Once the army left, these acres returned quickly to their original primeval state, and today nothing remains to mark the site of this large installation.

Camp Blanding, which had once been billed as the fourth largest city in the Sunshine State and sprawled over 170,000 acres, was reduced in size to a mere 30,000 acres, and its permanent cadre was reduced to a handful. Today, Camp Blanding is home to the Florida National Guard and occasional special training missions by other American forces. Nearby Starke, which had experienced rapid growth in development, quietly returned to the small town it previously had been. All of the crime and sleazy businesses that had once marked the course of "Boomtown Road" disappeared. The hustle and bustle of the boom-time era was quickly replaced by the placidity of a small town in rural Florida with little to distinguish it from hundreds of other rural towns.

Drew Field and Hillsborough Airfield returned to civilian control. Drew Field emerged in the postwar period as Tampa International Airport, while Hillsborough Airfield was gradually abandoned; the site of the base is now shared by residential housing, small businesses, Busch Gardens and the University of South Florida. Across Tampa Bay, Pinellas Airfield took on a postwar identity as the Clearwater International Airport, large enough to handle most commercial planes. MacDill Field lived on, enjoying continued importance in the Korean conflict and the Cold War, and is currently the home to several important military commands. It is also an active air base.

Eglin and Tyndall Airfields, now designated as air force bases, remain in active service. Eglin is the center for weapons testing, while Tyndall is home to several training schools and hosts active squadrons of the latest fighters in the American inventory. Like their World War II predecessors, Eglin and Tyndall Air Force Bases are considered important contributors to the economy of Florida's poorest region.

Sarasota Airfield is now the Sarasota International Airport. Page Airfield in Fort Myers was returned to the city and evolved into its municipal airport. Nearby Buckingham Field is now a "fly-in" residential community. Small air force and naval bases in Cross City, Keystone Heights, Brooksville, Daytona Beach, DeLand, Punta Gorda, Naples, Ocala, Gainesville, Marianna, Orlando, Vero Beach, Melbourne, Lakeland, Green Cove Springs and Sebring met similar fates. Some, like Morrison Field in Palm Beach County and Pinecastle/McCoy Airfield (now Orlando International Airport) in Orlando, remained under military control and became important bases in the Cold War, only to be put on the chopping block by later reductions in force. Avon Park Army Airfield continues in existence today and is still an important bombing and weapons-testing range.

Outlying fields, which were staffed by small detachments, were frequently turned over to county or municipal authorities and continue to operate as small airports. Although it was devastated by a hurricane in September 1945 and closed for a short period, Homestead Army Airfield would be reopened as a major base during the Cold War.

Jacksonville NAS and Mayport Navy Station remain active today, although the reductions in American military forces during the past twenty years have seen the loss of some of the outlying fields that once made up important parts of these complexes. In Pensacola, the navy continues to use Pensacola NAS as its primary training base for naval aviators, but it, too, has seen a dramatic reduction in the number of personnel stationed there. The Banana

River NAS was closed after the war but immediately reopened as the Long Range Missile Testing Range, where captured German- and American-developed rockets could be fired over the vast stretches of open ocean. It later underwent a metamorphosis and emerged as Patrick Air Force Base, which it remains today.

The super-secret "Station J" at Jupiter Inlet was closed and the facility turned over to the Coast Guard. The navy's Underwater Training Team base in Fort Pierce also closed its doors, and its training programs were transferred to California and Hawaii.

Although the military rapidly closed bases and abandoned them at the end of the war, there are still enough federal installations remaining, including the civilian-run National Aeronautics and Space Administration facility at Cape Canaveral, to have a significant impact on Florida's economy. A legacy of the war, they are but a small part of the change that the war brought to the Sunshine State. World War II was Florida's defining moment.

RECOMMENDED
READING

T he scope of Florida's contributions to training soldiers and sailors for
duty in World War II and the activities of the men and women in the
armed forces of the United States within the boundaries of the Sunshine
State are so immense that the complete story would take volumes to detail.
We have attempted to present an overall picture, but even that is a daunting
task. We recommend that the interested reader who is eager to know more
about a particular aspect of the involvement of Floridians and the Sunshine
State in this conflict read the books listed below. Even then, it is likely that
some important element will be omitted.

Billinger, Robert D., Jr. *Hitler's Soldiers in the Sunshine State: German POWs in
Florida*. Gainesville: University Press of Florida, 2000.

De Quesada, A.M. *The Royal Air Force Over Florida*. Charleston, SC: Arcadia
Publishing, 1998.

———. *World War II in Tampa Bay*. Dover, NH: Arcadia Publishing, 1997.

Freitus, Joseph, and Anne Freitus. *Florida: The War Years 1938–1945*. Niceville,
FL: Wind Canyon Publishing, 1998.

Gannon, Michael. *Operation Drumbeat: The Dramatic True Story of Germany's First U-boat Attacks along the American Coast in World War II.* New York: HarperCollins, 1991.

Homan, Lynn M., and Thomas Reily. *Wings Over Florida.* Charleston, SC: Arcadia Publishing, 1999.

Kleinberg, Eliot. *War in Paradise: Stories of World War II in Florida.* Cocoa: Florida Historical Society Press, 1999.

Largent, Will. *RAF Wings Over Florida: Memories of World War II British Air Cadets.* West Lafayette, IN: Purdue University Press, 2000.

Mormino, Gary Ross. *Hillsborough County Goes to War: The Home Front, 1940–1950.* Tampa, FL: Tampa Bay History Center, 2001.

Shettle, M.L., Jr. *Florida's Army Air Fields of World War II.* Bowersville, GA: Schaetel Publishing Co., 2009.

———. *United States Naval Air Stations of World War II.* Vol. 1. Bowersville, GA: Schaetel Publishing Co., 1995.

Smith, W. Sanford. *Camp Blanding: Florida Star in Peace and War.* Fuquay-Varina, NC: Research Triangle Publishing, Inc., 1998.

Taylor, Robert A. *World War II in Fort Pierce.* Charleston, SC: Arcadia Publishing, 1999.

Wynne, Lewis N., ed. *Florida at War.* St. Leo, FL: St. Leo College Press, 1993.

ABOUT THE AUTHORS

D r. Nick Wynne retired in 2008 from his post as executive director of
the Florida Historical Society. After obtaining his PhD in history, Dr.
Wynne taught college history at the University of South Florida. He has
published several books on Florida history, many of them with Arcadia,
including *Tin Can Tourists of Florida, Florida in the Civil War, Florida's Antebellum
Homes* and *Golf in Florida*. Since 1996, he has served as executive director
of the Florida Historical Library Foundation. He is an active lecturer
who has given 450 presentations and speeches in the past five years and
more than one hundred television and radio interviews. In addition, he
has secured more than $8 million in grants during the past twenty years.
He is a member of the Southern Historical Association, the American
Historical Association, the Florida College Teachers of History, the Georgia
Association of Historians and, of course, the Florida Historical Society. He
currently resides in Rockledge, Florida (near Cocoa Beach).

R ichard Moorhead has worked with Dr. Wynne on two books in the
past (*Paradise for Sale* and *Golf in Florida*). Prior to founding Richard
Moorhead & Associates, LLC, a medical sales, sales management and
marketing executive search firm, Moorhead was an integral part of the field
sales management team of Ethicon, Inc., a Johnson & Johnson company, for

over thirty-one years. He is a past member of the board of directors of the Florida Historical Society and is on the board of directors of the Historic Rosseter House Foundation in Eau Gallie, Florida. He and his wife reside in Winter Park, Florida.

Visit us at
www.historypress.net